"To be super successful, read *45 Things You Do That Drive Your Boss Crazy*. You will understand how to do the things that will drive your boss to promote you, give you a raise, have your future earning power expanded, and have a better life and future for yourself and your company by creating massive ...

—Mark Victor Hansen, cocreator, #1 *New Yo...* Chicken Soup for the Soul®, and coauthor *Code* and *The One Minute Millionaire*

"Reading this book might just triple your chances of being promoted."

—Tom Rath, bestselling author of *How Full Is Your Bucket?* and *Vital Friends*

"*45 Things You Do That Drive Your Boss Crazy* is like an armchair coach in a book. Anita Bruzzese not only identifies where our blind spots may be, but she also provides us with clear strategies for addressing them. A must-read for everyone!"

—Judith E. Glaser, CEO, Benchmark Communications, Inc., and author of *Creating We* and *The DNA of Leadership*

"Anita Bruzzese presents her readers with rare gifts: the tools and the coaching to take control of their own careers. Employees will prosper and bosses will smile wherever *45 Things You Do That Drive Your Boss Crazy* is required reading."

—Mark Wiskup, author of *Presentation S.O.S.*

"Peter Drucker once told me that half the leaders he met did not need to learn what to do—they needed to learn what to stop doing. This is a wonderful 'what to stop doing' guide. Practical, useful, and fun, it provides great coaching for employees of all levels."

—Marshall Goldsmith, top executive coach and author of *What Got You Here Won't Get You There*

45 Things You Do That Drive Your Boss Crazy*

*And How to Avoid Them

Anita Bruzzese

A PERIGEE BOOK

A PERIGEE BOOK
Published by the Penguin Group
Penguin Group (USA) Inc.
375 Hudson Street, New York, New York 10014, USA
Penguin Group (Canada), 90 Eglinton Avenue East, Suite 700, Toronto, Ontario M4P 2Y3, Canada
(a division of Pearson Penguin Canada Inc.)
Penguin Books Ltd., 80 Strand, London WC2R 0RL, England
Penguin Group Ireland, 25 St. Stephen's Green, Dublin 2, Ireland (a division of Penguin Books Ltd.)
Penguin Group (Australia), 250 Camberwell Road, Camberwell, Victoria 3124, Australia
(a division of Pearson Australia Group Pty. Ltd.)
Penguin Books India Pvt. Ltd., 11 Community Centre, Panchsheel Park, New Delhi—110 017, India
Penguin Group (NZ), 67 Apollo Drive, Mairangi Bay, Auckland 1311, New Zealand
(a division of Pearson New Zealand Ltd.)
Penguin Books (South Africa) (Pty.) Ltd., 24 Sturdee Avenue, Rosebank, Johannesburg 2196,
South Africa

Penguin Books Ltd., Registered Offices: 80 Strand, London WC2R 0RL, England

While the author has made every effort to provide accurate telephone numbers and Internet addresses at
the time of publication, neither the publisher nor the author assumes any responsibility for errors, or for
changes that occur after publication. Further, the publisher does not have any control over and does not
assume any responsibility for author or third-party websites or their content.

45 THINGS YOU DO THAT DRIVE YOUR BOSS CRAZY

Copyright © 2007 by Anita Bruzzese
Cover art by CSA Images
Cover design by Charles Bjorklund
Text design by Tiffany Estreicher

All rights reserved.
No part of this book may be reproduced, scanned, or distributed in any printed or electronic form with-
out permission. Please do not participate in or encourage piracy of copyrighted materials in violation of
the author's rights. Purchase only authorized editions.
PERIGEE is a registered trademark of Penguin Group (USA) Inc.
The "P" design is a trademark belonging to Penguin Group (USA) Inc.

First edition: February 2007

Perigee trade paperback ISBN: 978-0-399-53317-4

An application to register this title for cataloging has been submitted to the Library of Congress.

PRINTED IN THE UNITED STATES OF AMERICA

10 9 8 7 6 5 4 3 2 1

Most Perigee Books are available at special quantity discounts for bulk purchase for sales promotions,
premiums, fund-raising, or educational use. Special books, or book excerpts, can also be created to fit
specific needs. For details, write: Special Markets, The Berkley Publishing Group, 375 Hudson Street,
New York, New York 10014.

650.13
os
o = 8114459i

Acknowledgments

I once had a boss who told me publishing is often like giving birth. After having two children, I can tell you that giving birth is easier.

Writing is something that comes naturally to me, and something I love to do. But putting a book together takes a village, and I would not have been able to do it without the support—both professional and personal—of many people. First, my thanks to my friend and colleague Joanne Gordon, who encouraged me from the beginning and brainstormed and proofread early drafts. She not only gave me confidence to write this book, but offered lots of good advice and ideas. Second, I want to thank my agent, Stephanie Kip Rostan, who I affectionately call my master sergeant in book boot camp. She got me in fighting shape, always with encouragement and a little tough love thrown in. Third, my editor at Perigee, Marian Lizzi, who "got" the book from the beginning, and whose steady hand made this book even better. Fourth, my editor at Gannett News Service, Craig Schwed, who has always believed in my column and encouraged and supported my efforts.

Finally, I must thank the man who always makes me feel like the luckiest girl in the world. My husband, Len Bruzzese, who never loses faith in me and what I can do no matter how nuts I get. This book is dedicated to him and, of course, my boys, Nicholas and Ethan. Both make me proud every day.

This book would not exist if not for the hundreds of readers of my column who have shared their stories with me over the years, and an equal number of professionals who have shared their insight and wisdom. All of you have my respect and thanks.

Contents

Part Three
Snippy, Snotty and Socially Stunted: Bosses Don't Give Great Projects to Those Who Can't Play Nice and Get Along with Others

Part Four
Clueless in Seattle . . . and Cleveland . . . and Topeka . . . Bosses Don't Give Leadership Roles to Those Who Lack Maturity and Common Sense......149

Part Five
Sis, Boom, Bah! Failure to Give Full Support to Your Employer Says You're Not Ready for an Investment of Time and Resources.................201

45 Things You Do That Drive Your Boss Crazy

Introduction

L et's get this straight right off the bat: Bosses do not hire you to fire you.

It costs money to recruit and train someone, from the lowest position at a company to the top brass. It takes time and energy away from current employees every time someone has to show a new worker where the bathroom is or how to use the computer system.

So, it makes sense that your boss hires you to keep you. But after nearly twenty years of covering the workplace as a journalist, I think we have a problem.

Based on hundreds of letters I have received through my syndicated workplace column for Gannett News Service and USAToday .com, and hundreds of interviews I have done with company managers and career experts, something is seriously wrong here, folks.

The reason I say that is because I'm always getting letters from employees who are bewildered—*hurt*—that things have gone wrong or are going wrong in their careers. They don't understand it, they tell me. Why are they not successful at work? Why did the boss give them a poor performance evaluation? Why did they get passed over for the promotion or the raise?

The answer is usually the same: Because they didn't do what the boss wanted them to. (Duh.) And this, I have found, seems to confound many people. (Double duh.)

Let me be clear here: A boss expects you to be the best and the brightest you can be. That means you can't cut corners, or try to "get by," or whine about what you deserve. Bosses give you a paycheck and they expect certain things—many of which they do not believe they should have to tell you. That doesn't mean you won't get the training you need for certain tasks, but it does mean that you've got to stop making some pretty dumb workplace blunders.

It's sort of like the robin that came to my house last spring. Not unusual, of course. But this robin had a problem. He continually flew himself—full tilt—into my window.

This was alarming at first. I worried the poor bird would at least break a wing, and at worst kill himself. I wanted to help but didn't know what to do.

So I watched helplessly as the bird flew over and over into my window. It happened about every ten minutes for a couple of hours. He would sit in a nearby tree, fly into the window, then return to the tree.

Unfortunately, not only was this disturbing to watch such a misguided bird, but it seemed the impact would literally jar the poop out of him. My window was covered with bird droppings and the bird showed no sign of stopping.

But finally, it did stop. He simply flew away, leaving me no wiser as to his reasoning.

The next morning at daybreak, I was awakened by a thumping

noise. Every few minutes it sounded as if something would hit the side of the house, then stop. After lying there bleary-eyed for about ten minutes, I got a sneaking suspicion of what it might be.

The robin was back, and this time, he stayed. After a couple of weeks, after placing netting over the windows to try to keep him away, I was nearly crazed with that stupid bird. He was no longer a beautiful harbinger of spring but a nasty piece of ruffled feathers who was covering all my windows with poop, driving me from bed in the early hours and just driving me mad the rest of the time.

Finally, for no reason that I know of, he left for good. I don't know if the other robins did a kind of "robin intervention" to correct his self-destructive tendencies or he simply tired of the window assault and left.

Just like that bird, people in the workplace do things that make no sense and end up hurting themselves and driving those around them whacko. You may or may not be as stubborn as this bird, but I'll bet you have some bad habits that could be cleaned up.

My Milk Crate Overflows

I've covered the workplace from all its angles and bends. After all, I'm an employee myself. I work for a living and have since I was fifteen. I've even been an employer, subcontracting out work for various projects. As a business journalist, I've interviewed hundreds of top managers and workplace experts. I've heard from readers of my syndicated newspaper column on workplace issues over the years who ask me everything from how they can get along better with coworkers to what color they should paint the spare bedroom in their house.

When I was mulling over the writing of this book, I put a plastic milk crate under my desk. I thought I would place in it anything I found that showed me folks in the workplace just weren't getting it and were making some real career blunders over and over. In a couple of months that milk crate was overflowing. Surveys, news clippings and research reports were piled to the top.

One of the reports showed that the CEO of Boeing, Harry C. Stonecipher, was forced to resign after his romantic affair with a female executive was discovered. Stonecipher, who was married, was brought on board to help reestablish the global reputation of the company. Written communications at work from Stonecipher to the woman confirmed that an affair was ongoing.

Another newspaper clipping showed that Jeremy Wright, who sold the first blog, the Google IPO and Lemmings Online, was fired for blogging on the job. When I consulted his blog I found that he had written that he was fired for "divulging company secrets in a private space."

OK, so it became pretty darn clear to me that if some of the most highly trained, experienced employees were still screwing up, then there had to be plenty of others. I started to think about why mistakes were being made and began to see a picture emerge: employees and their bosses simply were not on the same page—and some didn't even appear to be in the same book.

Based on interviews with hundreds of people in the workplace over the years, I believe part of the problem is that employees often have the mind-set that since "everyone" spends time goofing off at work, or "everyone" gossips, or "everyone" is rude these days—it's really OK to do those things. The boss doesn't really care since "everyone" does it, the thinking seems to be.

But the truth is, the boss does care, and he believes employees should too. He further believes that correct behavior should be a given in the workplace. He doesn't believe he should have to lecture or cajole employees into behaving properly—he's not your teacher or your friend or your family. He is your boss and you are the employee. When your behavior shows that you don't get that— well, it drives him *crazy*.

The Employee/Employer Contract

When you interview for a job, you are questioned about your skills and experience and are finally chosen as the best person for the job over other applicants. That means an employer has invested in you before you even do a lick of work by:

* Advertising the job through newspapers, magazines and on-line sites

* Paying headhunter fees

* Putting you on the payroll

* Establishing security passwords and computer access

* Leasing for you the needed equipment such as pagers, cell phones and cars

* Taking current employees away from their jobs to interview you, answer questions and give you a facility tour

Then once you begin work, there are the weeks and months of training required to get you up to speed on everything from computers to client relations to future projects. It's been estimated by experts that you're not even contributing 50 percent until you've been on the job for about twelve weeks.[1] As for the employee you replace? It's estimated that when a worker leaves a company it costs an employer about 50 to 200 percent of that person's annual salary in terms of lost experience and abilities.[2]

So you see, the boss, from the moment you accept the job, has a big investment in you. He wants to see you succeed not only because a financial commitment has been made but because your success means his success. Period.

That's why bosses get more than a little frustrated when employees do stupid things. Like showing up for the first day of work with bright orange hair after being hired with perfectly nice brown hair. It's the kind of thing, you see, that gets a boss upset with you before you've even taken your first lunch break. Further, bosses don't like it when you get emotional and start crying or yelling when you have a crappy day. Such behavior makes them uncomfortable, and bosses eventually get rid of anything that makes them uneasy.

Keep in mind that bosses have bosses. That means they have their own pressures to put up with and the last thing they want to do is stop their own work and deal with an employee problem. Employee problems slow them down, add to their stress and generally make them cranky. Not the happy place where most people want their bosses to reside.

It's also important to remember that bosses today must deal

---

[1] William G. Bliss, president of Bliss & Associates, Inc., www.isquare.com/turnover.cfm

[2] http://sbinformation.about.com/od/hiringfiring/a/reduceturnover.htm

with employees who believe that since they aren't guaranteed a job for thirty years anymore, they aren't required to have any kind of loyalty to a company or a boss. Bosses face a world where employees are continually lost to competitors, better jobs or self-employment. They often are responsible for far-flung employees, telecommuting workers and employees who don't use English as their native tongue.

That's why they do not want to spend more dollars and time educating you about issues that they believe you should already know (such as orange hair). They don't have time to write a book of rules such as "don't wear your pajamas to work," or "don't talk on your cell phone during meetings," because they think you should already know that stuff (some of you do, some of you don't).

But I do have the time to write down the rules. At the same time, I want you to know *why* the rules are important and *why* they matter to the boss. I have never liked the "because I said so" response, so in this book you're going to finally understand and remember not only the rules but *why* they are rules in the first place.

It's time to grab your career with both hands and take responsibility for making it a success. Employers want you to be successful because your success means their success. I want you to be a smart employee, because then you won't write me those same, sad letters—or end up in my milk crate. And above all, you should want to do well in your job for any number of reasons, not excluding a steady paycheck.

I know that it can be overwhelming to know what to do and when to do it, but that reasoning can quickly turn into an excuse. It's easier after all to just throw up your hands and admit defeat to information overload. But why ignore information that can help you earn more money, be more successful, be more satisfied and lose weight (OK, so maybe not that)?

As you read this, remember that knowledge is power. With the right information—information your boss wants you to know and understand—you can be a much happier and productive employee. And the best part? It's not hard. So, let's get started!

Part One

Bad Attitudes, Dumb Moves and Dirty Jokes: Bosses Don't Promote Employees Who Make Them Feel Uncomfortable

Some of the most disconcerting letters I have received in writing a workplace column have to do with relationships at work. The reason I say this is because these letters are often dripping with drama—from the worker who believes a colleague is stealing her soda from the office refrigerator out of pure spite, to the employee who makes judgments about another worker based on gender and race.

Everyone—and I mean everyone—believes it is someone else's fault. I receive copies of court transcripts, employment records, memos, letters, etc., all claiming to be evidence that a problem at work is definitely, positively, someone else's fault. It's disturbing the level of dislike these people express for others in their workplace. It cannot, I believe, be a healthy environment and certainly must be one where workers would find it difficult to be very productive or effective.

You can then understand why bosses dislike having to deal with employees who behave as if they're still second-graders on the school playground. Managers do not want to tell Sharlene that Darlene thinks she's snippy. They do not want to have to intervene in disputes over whose turn it is to clean the office refrigerator. They greatly dislike having discussions with a worker about improper personal behavior, especially if it prompts temper tantrums, crying jags or whining fits from the employee.

Bosses know that an employee who causes friction at work or who behaves inappropriately and unprofessionally can have an adverse impact on others, and that's something they won't tolerate for long.

Research by Christine Pearson, a management professor at the University of North Carolina at Chapel Hill's Kenan-Flagler Business School, found that uncivil behavior among workers that caused strife included the following: sending a nasty or demeaning note, making accusations about a lack of knowledge, undermining credibility in front of others and being shouted at. Her study of 775 respondents found that 53 percent said they lost work time worrying about the incident or future interactions, while 46 contemplated changing jobs to avoid the instigator. Another 37 percent said they believed their commitment to the organization declined.

So if the company's bottom line takes a hit because workers are behaving inappropriately, you can bet the boss is looking to put a stop to it. Why? Because his success is tied to a company's success. The boss will find ways to remove what he considers to be the source of the problem, because that's what is best for everyone. But mostly he sees it as being good for him. He puts up with enough crap, and he believes that he shouldn't have to deal with constant moronic or idiotic behavior from an employee.

Get the picture? You mess with the boss's head by having a pissy attitude, embarrass him by behaving unprofessionally or tick him off by offending others and you are *so* not moving up the career ladder.

1. Treating the Office Like It's Your Love Shack

Dear Anita,
I was recently caught by my boss with a coworker's tongue in
my mouth and now my boss's face turns red whenever I make
eye contact with her. How can I alleviate her embarrassment
over a little kissing?
Puckering Pam

Dear Pam,
Your boss's face is probably not red with embarrassment, but
with anger. Your lapse in good judgment in the workplace by
canoodling with a coworker not only speaks to your lack of
professionalism, but, my God!! Under fluorescent lighting??
What were you thinking?
Anita

It's inevitable that since we spend an average of nearly 2,000 hours a year at work that we're going to form attachments to the folks we work with. Whether it's friendships or romances, we often find our personal and professional lives merging.

In fact, a survey by Careerbuilder.com found that 56 percent of employees have dated a coworker and one in four has dated someone higher up.

But nothing makes a manager reach for the antacid faster than an office romance. And it's not because he or she doesn't believe in true love. It's the end of true love—the lovers' spats, the jealous fits and the silent, angry glares—that makes a boss feel like Cupid's arrow just hit him in his nether regions.

How bad can it get? I will never forget the night my husband called me from work to tell me of an office romance gone sour.

"I thought a dog had gotten trapped here in the building," he began. "I just heard this awful howling noise, and everyone started looking around for this dog that seemed to be hurt or something."

But it wasn't a dog. It was a woman who had just gotten dumped by her boyfriend/coworker and was venting her displeasure in a stairwell that served as a perfect echo chamber. Imagine if you will, how awkward and embarrassing it was not only for the participants in this little romantic tangle but anyone within howling distance that day.

Still, office romances are going to happen. In fact, my husband and I met on the job so I'm not saying they should be forbidden. But I am a big believer in discretion. When you become involved with someone at work it doesn't just affect two people, and that is what concerns employers.

My husband and I worked about four feet from one another, and when it was clear that our friendship was going to take a romantic turn, we mapped out a battle plan.

While "battle plan" may seem a bit harsh, we didn't think so at the time. We worked in a newsroom—and journalists are the most notorious bunch of snoops and gossips around. They have been trained to be inquisitive and never to overlook any hint of a good story. And nothing is juicier than an office romance, so we knew that we couldn't leave anything to chance.

We had seen other workplace couples fall in and out of love and we knew that it could be a messy business. The goo-goo eyes they made at each other in the early stages of the attraction made everyone uncomfortable. And, if they weren't getting along—watch out. We saw coworkers put in the awkward position of trying to remain neutral through the couples' huffy silences and snide comments.

But back to my story: We managed to date secretly without anyone having a clue of what was going on. By the time my husband and I became engaged to be married, I had left the job and no longer worked with him. So the day he announced he was getting married, there were more than a few stunned expressions on the faces of some of the toughest, most tenacious journalists in the business.

"*Who* are you marrying?" they asked him.

When he told them, the expressions changed to anger and disbelief. They were, as a group, downright peeved that they had failed to spot the romance going on right under their noses. They began to search their memories, looking for signs they missed. Yes, sometimes they missed evidence that we were spending a lot of time together, but for the most part they were clueless.

We considered it, as a couple, one of our finest moments. (And yes, after the shock wore off they were genuinely happy for us.)

You may wonder how we kept our relationship private and why we did so.

The why:

★ We both considered our careers to be important, and we wanted to be seen as giving 100 percent when on the job—not distracted by a personal relationship.

★ We had both seen office romances and didn't like the "fishbowl" in which these couples were forced to exist. People are innately curious about others' private lives and they can't help but speculate about what is happening—every day.

★ We believed strongly that our personal lives were no one else's business. We knew that if the relationship was to stand a chance at developing it needed to be between two people and not a team sport. It cannot be discounted that workers sometimes like to meddle in office romances, which is not necessarily a good thing for a relationship.

★ Be it fair or unfair, we agreed that because I was female I would likely take the brunt of any gossip. In a world where women constantly struggle to gain equality, I knew I didn't need any additional hurdles.

★ We knew that any conversation we had—whether it was work related or not—would cause eavesdropping and speculation. We didn't constantly want to be looking over our shoulders wondering who was trying to hear some private tidbit.

If you decide a workplace romance is your heart's desire, then you need to use some workplace savvy in order to make sure that you don't come away with only regrets. You need to:

★ Behave discreetly. It's critical that no personal e-mails or phone calls should be sent between employees, especially those involved romantically. Remember in the introduction how I told you Boeing CEO Harry C. Stonecipher was forced to resign after his fling with a female executive in the company? Other Boeing officials found out about the affair between the married CEO and the woman when they got an anonymous tip that included written communication between the two lovers.

And here's something else to think about: At a time when companies struggle to put an ethical face on business after scandals at places such as Enron, Tyco and WorldCom, there is little tolerance for romances that may show "poor judgment" by a worker. All the more reason to behave discreetly and choose liaisons carefully. According to the Society for Human Resource Management, 81 percent of human resource professionals said they consider workplace romances dangerous because they could lead to conflict within the organization.

★ Keep away from the usual haunts. Everyone from work tends to hang out in certain places, especially at lunch and after work. Avoid them. Try to cut down on the chances of running into people from work by visiting new locations.

★ Remain friendly. If you go to lunch, invite others along and still go out with the gang after work sometimes. This cuts down on any suspicion that you're "sneaking away" from others to be alone.

★ No PDA. No kissing, no holding hands, no longing looks in one another's eyes. That's the stuff that gets you caught right away. Public displays of affection are never a good idea if you're hoping to be discreet.

Of course, all the points I described above may be different if one of you supervises the other. If that is the case, find out whether the company allows such relationships. Some have strict policies against them because they can lead to charges of sexual harassment. The important thing in any workplace romantic relationship is to go into it with your eyes wide open. Both people should agree on some "ground rules" that will provide a way to maintain professional integrity and personal peace.

2. Punching the Soda Machine When You're Stressed Out and Ticked Off

The first time I witnessed a physical, angry reaction in the workplace was when I was in college. Our campus newspaper office was across the hall from a couple of vending machines. One of the reporters for the newspaper was known to be a little volatile, but we all just sort of tolerated him. After all, he was one of the brightest, most tenacious reporters we had, so we just looked upon his angry outbursts (which usually involved a lot of curse words) as something we had to put up with.

Then one night his temper boiled out of control and he started prowling the newsroom like a caged rottweiler. He finally charged into the hallway, startling some innocent student intent on getting herself a Diet Coke.

BAM!

In one swift move this angry guy punched the Coke machine square in the "no deposit, no return" sign. The other student, still clutching her change, quickly backed away and hit the stairs at a trot.

BAM! BAM!

Again, the soda machine was taking abuse, this time as our angry colleague gave it a few swift kicks.

After another couple of right-cross jabs, he stopped. Chest heaving and muttering under his breath, he left the building.

We all sort of laughed it off, but I remember being concerned. First, because it was unsettling to see someone hit an innocent soda machine. Second, because I was worried about what might set this guy off next. And what—or who—would be his next target? The copier? The candy machine? Me?

The guy soon left school and the next thing we heard he was in Special Forces for the U.S. military. And even though he was talented, I don't think any of us were sorry to see him go. He was unpredictable, and no one wanted to work with him for fear of what would set him off.

While his actions came years before the first employee went "postal" in this country, we now all unfortunately know that anyone who becomes verbally or physically aggressive at work is indeed something to be concerned about.

The U.S. Department of Labor (DOL) says that some two million Americans are the victims of workplace violence each year. Included: bites, squeezes (not the affectionate kind), punches, scratches, hits, kicks and beatings. The worst-case scenario, of course, is when an employee kills someone in the workplace. Unfortunately, it is a scenario that managers must keep in mind if you get ticked and throw your phone, kick a door or start yelling and cursing.

You may believe that your burst of temper or frustration isn't something to be concerned about. You are, after all, just frustrated and releasing a little steam. But the boss doesn't care if you're a card-carrying member of Amnesty International or walk in a PETA parade every year. He sees uncontrolled emotion as a potential danger and that's his signal to step in to talk to you, to keep a written record in your personnel file, or both.

This is partly because he is concerned about the safety of other workers (and himself), but also because most managers have received very direct instructions from the head honchos that they're supposed to keep close track of aggressive behavior. Workplace violence is estimated to cost employers $36 billion a year, according to the DOL, and employees who have been bitten or squeezed or injured in some way often require two to three days off to recover.

Further, companies are nervous about being taken to court if they ignore any potential violence. Courts have ruled that companies have a responsibility to take action to keep employees from being harmed, whether it's providing forklift safety training or preventing an employee from cursing out the receptionist.

So you see, while you may see your little snit fit as no big deal, the boss sees it as a potentially very big deal: absenteeism, lost productivity and lawsuits. All problems that any boss greatly dislikes.

Also keep in mind that once the boss writes down your little transgression—whether it's bashing a piece of machinery or jabbing a coworker in the arm—then there is written documentation that can lead to you being suspended or fired. At the very least, the boss may require you to take anger management classes, which many of your coworkers will find out about no matter how you try to keep it a secret.

So, if you feel frustrated or angry or have the urge to toss your chair through the window, there are some things you can do to get a handle on the situation.

The first is to recognize you have a problem. Most people can say, "This just isn't me. I'm not acting like myself." Sometimes a family member or friend will feel the same about your behavior and that's a real affirmation that something needs to be done. If you want to get the stress under control, try the following:

* Keeping a job journal. Document not only what happened at work that got under your skin, but how you handled it. Look for patterns of stress, connected to either a certain person, event or time of day. Make notes of how you believe you could have handled something better and alleviated some stress.

* Visit the doctor. Get a complete checkup. Stress often can trigger physical ailments and it's much more difficult to handle problems if you're physically not up to the challenge. Or it could be there is a physical cause for the mental anguish you're feeling.

* Move it. Working in cubicles or spaces where there is little chance to move around can lead to increased stress and frustration. Some people have even called it "desk rage" or "cubicle rage." Make it a priority to get away from your area several times a day to take the stairs to another floor and use the restroom, or walk down the hall to get a drink of water. Hand deliver a message to a coworker instead of phoning or sending an e-mail.

* Eat out. Try to never eat at your desk even if it means you take only twenty minutes and eat in the break room. If you don't want to talk to anyone, put on headphones and listen to a book on tape or relaxing music. The best idea is to take a walk at lunch or step outside the door for a breath of fresh

air. Remember: Bosses won't begrudge you some downtime and would rather you take it than risk blowing your cool because you're overworked and overstressed. Take a break when it's due.

★ Address personal concerns. It could be that your reaction to stress is erupting at work but it's really your personal life that is the cause of problems. Many human resource departments have resource lists for things like elder care, day care or community assistance programs to help employees. Ask for the most current employee benefits handbook so that you are familiar with all the services your company offers— many offer discounts to things like gyms or day care, or may provide some financial or family counseling through other sources. If you are a valued employee, bosses often are open to offering you some flexibility in your schedule to accommodate personal demands. The important thing is to identify where the stress is coming from and then find ways to alleviate it.

3. Goofing Off on a Business Trip

According to the National Business Travel Association (NBTA), more than $150 billion a year is spent on domestic business travel, which accounts for nearly one-third of all domestic travel. Nearly forty million Americans are hitting the road for business each year and that number is expected to grow.

It's no wonder, then, that we're all looking for a way to make our business travel misadventures pay off. So what if we fudge the expense account a little to pay for the wear and tear on our bodies and our psyches? We deserve it, don't we? And so what if we find time to unwind a little bit while we're on the road? We deserve to have fun, don't we?

Well, yes and no. Bosses know the demands of the road as well as anyone and they would agree an employee should find time to relax if the schedule permits. In a boss's mind, that would entail something like a nice dinner. Or maybe a movie. Perhaps a stroll through the city streets to take in the sights after a long meeting.

It does not, however, include things like partying in a coworker's room, getting looped at a bar, or generally making a horse's ass of yourself in front of clients, coworkers and half of Boston.

And here's why: Your workplace follows you. It doesn't matter that you've left the building; you are still on the company dime. You still have to abide by the same conduct you would if you were in that building.

That's why indiscreet behavior during business travel can still result in charges of sexual harassment. (If you're not sure what "indiscreet" means, just pretend your boss is sitting right beside you at all times. That should keep your behavior in check.)

"I do think a lot of behavior takes place on business trips that would never happen back at the office," says Charlotte Shelton, a management professor and frequent international business traveler. "People need to remember that they are ambassadors of their companies and behave accordingly."

Business travel often can lead to behavior problems just because it seems to be just one big, damn hassle after another. It's easier, after all, to call someone to your hotel room to deliver documents than try to speak in a crowded and noisy hotel lobby. But it's not a good idea because a hotel room, where you are out of sight of others, could set the stage for a sexual harassment charge.

It's also easy to let your guard down when you've been traveling because you're tired and more than a little punchy after crossing various time zones. You may start bad-mouthing a manager or another coworker to an associate or even to a complete stranger. You may decide you need a drink and hit the hotel or airport bar, which only makes your big mouth run more. And, gee . . . wouldn't the boss just think it was hilarious that you got bumped from your flight by the airline because you were so intoxicated? Or that a client happened to be in the same bar with you and overheard you—somewhere around your third martini—start saying nasty things about him?

That's why it's best to avoid situations that set the stage for problems. Stay away from clubs or the types of restaurants where the atmosphere is definitely partyville or romance friendly. If a coworker traveling with you wants to have a good time, try to arrange an outing to a ballgame, museum or local shops. If this isn't what the coworker had in mind, you always can claim you have more work to do and have a quiet dinner with a little HBO in your room.

Some other business-travel tips:

* Avoid dressing down. There's always a chance you could run into a colleague, a client or a company manager while on the road. While traveling on business, you are a representative of your boss and your company. Avoid wearing anything too sloppy or sexy while traveling. Try to stick to business casual or nicer.

* Don't flirt. No matter your marital state, it's best to avoid personal entanglements while on the road. Word will get back to your boss. "It's a small world after all" is more than an annoying song. Industry professionals are often a tight-knit bunch. They talk—and they'll especially talk if they catch you flirting. What's considered flirting? Touching someone of the opposite sex for more than a handshake, kidding in a sexual way, remarking on someone's looks, leaning in, etc. *You* know what flirting is.

* Don't go "out" too much. It's one thing to catch lunch with associates at a city's popular eatery. It's another thing to hit a city's attractions at every opportunity. The boss will wonder if you got any work done in between all your sightsee-

ing. If you want to play tourist, build in some personal vacation time after your work is done and you are off duty.

★ Be secure. Vital, secure information is often on your laptop or contained in files you carry with you while traveling. Never leave these items where they might be snatched—ask the hotel or convention site management for a secure place to store your belongings. Never count on a locked room or car to keep out a determined thief. The boss will be less than pleased to find out you lost track of confidential information because you were having a good time instead of taking care of business.

4. Earning a Reputation as a Whiner, Drama Queen or General Pain in the Neck

It often comes as a rude shock when we learn what others think of us at work. You may consider yourself passionate, for example. But guess what? In the eyes of others, you're a drama queen.

Maybe you consider yourself to be sensitive, concerned and empathetic. But others see you as a whiner.

Or maybe you think your nature is one of strength, committed to doing a job right and always willing to challenge opinions. Other people, however, consider you a pain in the neck.

And what other people think of you at work really matters. Because those perceptions wind their way up the food chain and land right on the boss's doorstep. She may not have a lot of daily contact with you, but others do. And what she hears from others is what she will take into account when she deals with you.

For example, say she decides to talk to you about a problem with a deadline. It seems the client wants the work done sooner and has made changes in the overall project. She wants your input about what you foresee as problems.

"OH. MY. GAWD!" you gasp, clutching your chest as if your heart might leap out and land on your laptop. "Are you kidding? What are we going to do? This is just awful!"

Now perhaps your next words will be: "Well, we'll just have to find a way to make this work."

But your boss is still stuck on the vision of your eyes bugging out, your eyebrows shooting to your hairline and your mouth gaping open like a landed halibut. And in her mind, she's thinking: "Yep. Guess everyone was right. Drama queen."

Fair? Maybe not. But you got that reputation somehow and now you're paying the price. Instead of the boss being impressed with your ability to get the job done she's wondering if smelling salts are available and if they still make fainting couches.

The same thing happens with whiners. Maybe you have said, "But *why* do I have to . . ." in the same tone as a five-year-old being told it's bedtime. Maybe you've moaned like you were having an appendicitis attack when the boss gave you an assignment. Maybe you didn't verbalize anything, but your huge sighs could be heard across the street.

Further, you often wring your hands, constantly discuss your physical state ("I'm so tired, stressed, depressed," etc.) and spend more time lamenting what you have to do rather than doing it. Is it any wonder that your reputation as a whiner is rock solid?

And finally, there is the general-pain-in-the-neck category. The specifics can differ depending on your behavior. But if you're a real pain, you can bet the boss will know it. She'll know it because she'll see the angry, agitated, disgusted and frustrated reactions you provoke in coworkers. She'll spot the fact that others don't seem to listen to you as much as they seem to just try to tolerate—or avoid—you.

The boss will understand that if others can barely stand you, the work will suffer. Workplaces depend on people cooperating with one another in order to be effective and productive, and your behavior can have an adverse impact. She also will be concerned that if you have a bad reputation and she ends up promoting you, employees may wonder if she's lost her mind.

Laura Shelton, a television reporter, says that a woman with a reputation as a "negative drama queen" was once promoted in her newsroom. "We all wondered, what is [the manager] thinking?" she recalls.

Shelton says that even though the woman ended up working out well in the new position, the initial impact was that some lost respect for the manager when the decision was made.

Let me give you another example of how your personal behavior can work against you. I once was employed at a company where one woman was such a pain that we all finally started closing our office doors as a way to bar her entry. (Sometimes it worked and sometimes it didn't. We all lived in fear that the next knock on our door would be her.)

Finally, a coworker took her aside and pointed out that her behavior (nitpicking something to death, working very slowly, constantly regaling us with the personal details of her crumbling marriage) was driving us bonkers. She looked bewildered. He decided to offer specific instances. At the end of the conversation, she was not angry. In fact, she thanked him for cluing her in. But in the coming days she changed her pain-in-the-neck behavior not one iota. We went back to huddling behind our doors. That is, until the boss began to question why we were all hiding as if Geraldo Rivera wanted an interview. A few comments here and there, and he got a very clear idea of who was causing his office to break down into a bunch of adults afraid to come out of their offices.

Within days he began "paper trailing" her—writing up offenses that ranged from missing deadlines to misfiling reports. Just a few weeks later, he had enough warnings to fire her.

Was this fair? Were the warnings against her nothing more than trumped-up charges to get rid of someone we all thought was a pain in the butt? I can't say for sure. But what I do know is that her behavior impacted us all, and the boss couldn't help but try to find out what was breaking down the morale and efficiency of his business.

"Perception is reality. It's very difficult for a boss to see you differently once you've been perceived a certain way," says Charlotte Shelton, a major university management professor. "It's going to make it tough on a manager to promote you because you've tied her hands with your reputation."

I'm not saying that you have to be palsy-walsy with your co-workers. Sometimes that's not possible because individual personalities can be so different. What I am saying is that it's important that you fit in as a member of the workplace team. If you get a reputation of being a whiner, a drama queen, or a pain in the neck, it's much harder to be thought of as an integral part of the overall effort. The boss did not hire you to exist in a vacuum. She hired you to work with others in a competent, constructive manner.

Still, you can make repairs even if you've gotten an unfavorable reputation. It's going to require proving day in and day out that you've changed your ways, and it may take some time, but it will be worth it if you truly seek workplace success. (And you can continue to be a pain in the butt, a whiner or a drama queen in your personal life if that's what you really want.)

Try to do the following:

* Take control. Did you ever consider that you became Scarlett O'Hara because you feel powerless and what you really need is a little more responsibility in your life? Maybe you seek excitement and when you don't get it, you decide to manufacture it through histrionics. Try getting involved in making more decisions, whether it's changing coffee vendors or volunteering to handle a difficult client.

* Be honest with yourself and others. Don't exaggerate when trying to get someone's attention. If people are not listening to you, consider that it's just bad timing rather than an indication that you need to ratchet up the drama or start whining.

* Become more self-sufficient. Crying for help when you don't really need it or overdramatizing an issue makes others feel manipulated and less inclined to trust you on other issues (remember the little boy who cried wolf?). Learn to stand on your own two feet and you'll find that when you really need help, others don't mind pitching in.

* Suck it up. If you're sick, stay home. Don't come to work and whine about it. If you've got personal issues, take care of them as privately as possible—sighing, moaning and complaining about your life should be shared with friends and family after work hours.

★ Lend a hand. The best way to stop thinking of yourself and your own problems is to offer aid to someone else. Help a coworker who is swamped, cover for someone who is on vacation or just clean out the office fridge. Remember that whining is reserved for those under age five.

★ Find professional help if you need it. Maybe the behavior you exhibit at work is a result of your upbringing or other circumstances. Maybe you were raised by a pack of wolves or hatched in a cabbage patch. Whatever. Most of your coworkers will be understanding—to a point. But when your little problems and peccadilloes start impacting their work, then they can become less accommodating. One of the best strategies for overcoming this reputation is to find a personal coach. This might be someone in your private or professional life, but it should be someone who has a reputation for integrity, honesty and hard work. Ask this person to help you review your behavior and areas where you might make improvements. My problem coworker was given a golden opportunity when a colleague presented the case that she needed to make some changes. But she blithely went on her own way—and that turned out to be right out the door.

5. Discussing Your Personal Beliefs at Work

Dear Anita,
I recently had my "Save the Wombats" T-shirt on at work, and one of the guys I work with said, "The only good wombat is the one I have for breakfast with my coffee." And he was serious! How can I continue to work with this immature moron?
Sunny

Dear Sunny,
The workplace is tough enough without dragging some poor Australian marsupial into the equation. When you bring your personal beliefs into a professional setting, you jeopardize the delicate balance of the working world's ecosystem. I advise you to save the wombats on your own time.
Anita

No one can dispute the fact that Americans are an opinionated bunch. Ask us anything from what is the best kind of ice cream to what really happened to Jimmy Hoffa, and you're going to get an earful.

But the personal opinions that may seem fairly harmless when being discussed with friends and family can quickly get out of control in the workplace. That's because in our private lives we often hang out with people who are like us, who share our same views. On the job, it's a whole different kettle of fish.

While Title VII of the Civil Rights Act of 1964 prohibits workplace discrimination based on religion, national origin, race, color or sex, Congress has failed as of this writing to pen something like: "No waving your personal beliefs at work like the checkered flag at a NASCAR race."

Under the law in other words, bosses aren't going to object to you observing your religious holidays or dress, and won't even flutter an eyelash if you're a practicing Wicca member. What bothers your boss, however, is when you engage others in discussions of issues that can turn the workplace into a WWE SmackDown.

He doesn't care if you don't eat meat but he doesn't want you preaching your views to the guy across the hall wolfing down a chili cheese dog. He doesn't care who you plan to vote for in the next election but he doesn't want you wearing that candidate's T-shirt to work, or covering your cubicle with little elephants or donkeys.

"You can really get disruptive when you're talking about your personal beliefs at work. Tempers will get raised, and people will be distracted from their work. Then the manager is going to have to clean up the mess. Plus, you may veer into an unlawful area if someone considers they're being harassed on a religious issue, for example," says Jeffrey Tanenbaum, a lawyer specializing in employment and labor.

Why are bosses more concerned than ever about personal hot button issues? Consider:

* On November 1, 2004, the websites of JohnKerry.com and GeorgeWBush.com each drew more than 300,000 U.S. visitors. More than half of the users of those sites were in the workplace.

* The Equal Employment Opportunity Commission received more than 2,500 complaints of religious discrimination in 2003, a surge of some 75 percent from 1993. Complaints included proselytizing to others at work.

* Political websites, which grew a whopping 400 percent from 2000 to 2004, "may cause a considerable drain on employee productivity" because peak usage hours are from 11 a.m. to 3 p.m., reports Websense.

Bosses see these kinds of numbers and know that employees are spending time at work feeding their personal interests instead of concentrating on their jobs. And while bosses aren't demanding that workers abandon personal beliefs, they would like employees to keep those issues out of the workplace.

"When people talk about their beliefs, it triggers strong emotions. They start battling people who don't believe as they do, and they get in an entrenched position," says Judith Glaser, CEO of a communications strategy company. "It raises a conflict situation—and most bosses are very conflict averse."

That means they don't want to fight battles they believe shouldn't be going on in the first place. So, here are some guidelines to keep your boss happy and your personal beliefs from interfering with your career success:

★ Be realistic. Not everyone shares your love of the wombats, and some might even hate them. It is not part of your job description to educate your workplace about why the little critters are important, the part they play in the marsupial world or how colleagues can contribute to the worldwide fund to save them.

★ Be discreet. This means that you leave at home T-shirts, bumper stickers and posters that declare your allegiance to a political party or any other organization you support. These little mementos are for your home, not your workspace. If you can't help yourself, wear your donkey boxers. It will be your little secret.

★ Keep it off company time. Don't make phone calls, use the Internet, the copier, the shredder, the pencil sharpener or the stapler for anything that smacks of personal business. Ask members of your group or organization to contact you at home.

★ Be cool. If someone at work tries to engage you in a discussion of your personal beliefs, or you don't agree with what was said and want to discuss it further, invite the person to call you at home or meet after work hours. If you don't want to get into it, just say, "I'd rather not."

I realize it may be tough for some people to quash their natural tendency to share their personal beliefs with everyone at work. As George Burns once said: "It's too bad the only people who know how to run the country are busy driving cabs and cutting hair." He could have added, "and standing around the water cooler at work."

6. Telling Dirty Jokes and Cussing on the Job

Most of us have experienced rude behavior in the workplace, from the guy who can burp the alphabet to the woman who eats other people's food from the office fridge. Annoying, yes. Rude, yes. But not something that can necessarily land the person in legal hot water.

The same cannot be said for swearing and dirty jokes at work. Those behaviors are not only rude but worrisome for bosses because they can lead to charges of sexual harassment.

Now, it's one thing to thing to slam your fingers in a drawer and give a startled "%$#$!" It's another to say, "Hey, Fred, can you hand me that $%# invoice from that #$%# customer?"

Sure, we're all adults and a little cussing will not make anyone turn to stone. But employees have been fired for cussing by bosses who have a zero-tolerance policy or little use for employees who channel Howard Stern. Bosses also fear what impact cussing and foul humor will have on others: A woman who worked for the television show *Friends* claimed in her sexual harassment lawsuit that profanity was part of the problem.[3]

Still, these days one person's idea of cursing may not be another's. For example, when I was growing up saying the word "suck" as in "you suck!" was something that would get a bar of Dial shoved in your mouth by your mom. But years ago I started hearing it used in everything from television sitcoms to vacuum cleaner commercials.

I e-mailed my sister: "Do you think 'suck' is still a bad word? What if one of my kids says it? Is that a soaping offense?"

After polling her friends, she e-mailed back: "Yes. The word 'suck' is bad. It should not be said."

That was several years ago, and things have changed. Most people no longer think of it as a bad word and use it freely. Still, the point is that some older workers—or clients—might still consider it offensive. Even your boss might consider the word "suck" OK until she finds out that customers or other workers don't care for it—then she's going to want you to clean up your mouth.

Remember, once you make someone else feel uncomfortable, then the boss starts to feel it too. And that, as I've pointed out, is a bad thing.

"I've found that the more sensitive a person is, the less likely he or she is to say that something offends them," says Linda Barrington, a research director and labor economist. "If the boss doesn't put a stop to it, then that person thinks the boss is in agreement with what is being said. So that's why the boss cares and wants it to stop."

To avoid problems:

---

[3] "Longing for a Cuss-Free Zone," *The New York Times*, July 31, 2005

* Always figure someone is eavesdropping. This is the best way I know to keep from telling even one little dirty joke at work. You know that nothing is secret in the workplace—there's a very good chance someone will overhear you, including the boss.

* Keep a "swearing" jar on a coworker's desk. Let the person have whatever money you put in it. Whenever you slip up and say a profanity at work, put in a dollar. (You may have to start with a quarter if you have an especially foul mouth.) This has been a tried-and-true method of parents everywhere who want to quit cussing in front of the kids.

* Think about why you do it. Why do you swear? Is it to get attention or to intimidate others? Turning the air blue will never make you seem tougher or smarter. In fact, your boss will probably think just the opposite.

* Consider your future. Before you tell that dirty joke or start swearing, think whether it's how you want to be remembered when that next promotion or opportunity comes along. Bosses have long memories—is that the perception you want them to carry?

7. Having Questionable Personal Integrity

Oprah Winfrey, never at a loss for words, says that "real integrity is doing the right thing, knowing that nobody's going to know whether you did it or not."

In the workplace, that means you don't goof around on the Internet when you're supposed to be working, you don't fudge your travel expense reports and you don't claim to be working from home when you're really watching DVDs with your cat.

If you do, however, it probably won't be a big surprise to folks you work with.

In fact, Ilene Gochman, author and sponsor of a study on employee attitudes, found that only 60 percent of 1,200 workers she polled "believed coworkers acted with honesty and integrity."[4]

Gochman says a "busybody" mentality at work is leading work-

[4] Reprinted with permission from "Work USA 2004: An Ongoing Study of Employee Attitudes and Opinions—Performance Management Summary" copyright © 2006 by Watson Wyatt Worldwide. For more information, visit www.watsonwyatt.com.

ers to watch one another's behavior more closely, getting downright peevish about other workers not doing what they promise.

"There are little cliques and favoritism that lead people to say their coworkers are not walking the talk," she says. "For example, some people may resent the worker with kids who gets off early while the others have to stay and work."

It's clear that all of these gripes are direct shots at personal integrity. Now I know most of you are saying, "Yeah, but why do I have to show integrity when the CEOs in this country are making off with millions and millions of dollars illegally? They don't have personal integrity, so why should I?"

Well, how about the fact that their actions have gotten them jail time? Their behavior has ruined not only their employees' lives but also their own. Their families are left to suffer the humiliation of watching these CEOs do the "perp walk" on national television. They are the butt of jokes on late-night television and the subject of many a Sunday sermon. They have left their children and grandchildren with a legacy of destruction and deceit.

Still want to jump off that bridge just because they did?

Let's hope not. Because Gochman's survey makes it clear that bosses are taking a higher moral ground. Specifically, some 72 percent of employees believe their immediate boss behaves with honesty and integrity.

So, if the boss behaves appropriately, then that means he expects the same of you. Let's consider some personal integrity issues and where you stand:

★ Lies. This can range from fibbing about why you were late to work to fudging your expense report. Lying is a way of controlling and manipulating people and situations. For many bosses, lying is grounds for firing you. Keep in mind that once a boss discovers—either on his own or through other workers—that you lie about even little stuff, he will start to wonder what else you lie about. Once you earn a boss's mistrust it will be hard to advance in your job—or even hang on to it.

★ Blame. Are you quick to blame someone else when something goes wrong? Do you spend more time covering your own behind instead of fixing the problem? Bosses don't appreciate workers using work time to play the blame game.

★ Sticky fingers. So, those envelopes, pens, pencils, scissors, etc., just fell into your backpack, huh? Absconding with company property is just like when you pilfered that pack of gum from the grocery store when you were a kid. Mom was smart enough back then to smack your hand before you got away with it. This time around, the boss will smack you with a pink slip and possible criminal charges.

★ Keeping your word. If you tell a coworker you will take care of something, then do it. "It's all an issue of fairness," Gochman says. "It's not fair that someone doesn't do the work she says she will."

★ Faking it. Let's say it's a nice day and you'd really like to hang out with your friends instead of working. You call in sick, never giving any thought to the fact that a coworker will have to work doubly hard to make up for your absence, or perhaps will have to give up a legitimate day off to cover for you. You not only are violating the employee/employer contract, but you're dumping extra work on other people through your own selfishness.

★ Hanging with the right people. My Italian grandmother-in-law used to say something like, "You lie down with dogs, you're going to get up with fleas." The Americanized version is something like: You are known for the company you keep. If you pal around with those at work who have less-than-stellar reputations of honesty and integrity, then you could be asking for trouble. Even if you don't pull some (or any) of the shenanigans they do, your reputation for personal integrity still will suffer. Look for those in the workplace who obviously have the respect of not only coworkers but the boss. These are the people you want to watch and learn from.

Part Two

Stupid, Sloppy or Sleepy: Bosses Get Rid of Employees with Too Many Bad Habits

Everyone has bad habits. But what your significant other is willing to put up with at home, your boss is not.

When you pick your teeth in public it is not just annoying, it's gross. Eating like a pig at a trough during a business lunch is nauseating. Your bad habit of interrupting everyone—even if it's out of enthusiasm—is rude.

Let me assure you, by the way, that these bad habits are not going unnoticed and are of real concern to your boss. Why? Because he fears others will hold him accountable for your crude ways.

And of special concern to your boss these days are the bad habits you have online. A majority of companies now monitor Internet use and company e-mail, and employees have received disciplinary actions for infractions—or have been fired outright.

Companies also are becoming increasingly tough on employees who blog about work, whether it's criticism of an employer or just describing the duties of a particular job. Employers that have fired people for blogging include Delta Air Lines, Wells Fargo, ESPN and the National Basketball Association.

While blogging and viewing porn at work are enough to get you fired, there are other offenses that won't—but still drive bosses nuts. People at work care *a lot* about what they consider to be rude, crude and socially unacceptable behavior on the job, whether it's leaving a mess in the lunchroom or putting up a Hooters poster in a cubicle. Perhaps it's because more employees work longer hours in tighter spaces, but it's getting testy out there. Nearly half of workers polled by OfficeTeam said the level of professional courtesy at work has decreased over the past five years, and bosses don't like that trend one bit. The bad habits of workers have the annoying habit of spilling over into a boss's realm, and that's not something he wants *his* bosses seeing.

What drives people crazy the most? Many of my letters from readers gripe about issues like the coworker who gabs for hours on the phone to friends and family, then takes a ninety-minute lunch followed by a thirty-minute personal grooming session. Some letters complain about coworkers forgetting the basic civilities such as saying "please" and "thank you."

Like you, I have witnessed firsthand some of the workplace incivility that seems to be spreading like a bad smell. In a sporting goods store, I watched as an employee tried to show a customer a new running shoe as another worker pushed a large clothing rack through the middle of the conversation. This worker never said "excuse me" as the customer and the other employee stumbled to get out of the way. This, of course, ticked off the employee trying to make the sale, who quickly made a sarcastic comment to the other worker. A snide comment was fired back, and so on and so on. You get the idea. The customer was put in the middle of a spat that could have been avoided with some common courtesy from both employees.

I know that bad habits can be hard to break. But if you don't break them, they grow in importance. They keep others—including the boss—focused on what you do wrong instead of what you do right. So, if it takes an etiquette course to improve your manners, if it takes a personal shopper to spiff up your appearance, if it takes additional education to improve your writing or speaking skills— do it. It will be one of the best investments you make in your career and, more important, in yourself as a human being.

8. Blogging About Your Job

Dear Anita,
Recently, my boss made a stupid decision on a new product
we're developing and I think it will cost us millions. Thank
God, I can vent to you—and to my blog. It really has saved my
sanity, being able to journal about my frustration. I recom-
mend it to anyone who has to work for an idiot.
Blog Happy

Dear Happy,
I think writing down your frustrations and concerns is an ex-
cellent idea, but not on the Internet for billions to see! You
can get fired for stuff like that, and plenty of people have.
Stick to the pen and paper, and possibly, invisible ink.
Anita

I want to make this perfectly clear: If you want to hang on to
your job, don't write about it in your personal online diary. Because just as sure as you do, the boss is gonna find out, and as the
old saying goes: Your ass is grass, and he's the lawnmower.

"It's a bad idea anytime you decide to go online and say bad things about your company or the people who work there," says Gregg Lemley, a lawyer specializing in such issues. "Casting an employer in a bad light can mean you will face disciplinary action, and that could mean you can be fired."

You may think that casting a company or management in a bad light means you call them low-down, scum-sucking rodents with the collective IQ of lint. Not so. Workers have been dismissed for being sarcastic about employee recognition awards, or discussing what projects they are working on. And, in case you're thinking that no one could ever find out about your blogging since there's an estimated eight million blogs[5] (and growing) on the Internet, think again. Many a stupefied employee has found out the hard way that their "anonymous" postings have been discovered.

Under the pseudonym of "Sarcastic Journalist," Rachel Mosteller wrote this in her personal blog: "I really hate my place of employment. Seriously. Okay, first off. They have these stupid little awards that are supposed to boost company morale. So you go and do something 'spectacular' (most likely, you're doing your JOB) and then someone says 'Why golly, that was spectacular,' then they sign your name on some paper, they bring you some chocolate and some balloons.

"Okay two people in the newsroom just got it. FOR DOING THEIR JOB."

While Mosteller didn't give her real name or her company (*The Durham (NC) Herald-Sun*), her supervisors and coworkers were

---

[5] Pew Internet & American Life Project

aware of her postings. The day after writing this gem in her blog, she was fired.

For those who are indignantly aquiver over what they consider to be their right to free speech, companies will argue just as fervently that they have a right to protect their reputation in the marketplace. That means if they are portrayed unflatteringly in a blog, or if they believe company information is being shared with the cyber world without their authorization, they will put a stop to it— even if that means firing an employee.

What's the lesson here? If you are a blogger, it's best to stick with writing about your family vacation, the frustrations of trying to train a new puppy and whether orange really is the new pink.

9. Having Poor Writing and Spelling Skills

No one is perfect. Everyone makes writing, spelling and grammatical errors. Even the pros:

* In a headline from the *Asheville (NC) Citizen-Times*, there was this headline: "Weather watchers keep eyes on the sky for meteorologists."

* In the *Olympian* in Olympia, Washington, a headline read: "Some adults grow into blemishes."

Journalists, like anyone else, have a lot of rules that they try to follow to eliminate as many errors as possible. One of the greatest inventions for everyone has to be the spell-check on computers. This has reduced the number of spelling errors greatly, although it doesn't eliminate all problems. For example, I was in an ice cream store and a sign generated by a computer said: "We do not except credit cards." The computer didn't know the word should be "accept," not "except." To the computer, all the words were spelled correctly. It was the computer user who was in error.

And he or she was not alone. According to the National Commission on Writing, up to one-third of employees at blue-chip companies do not have adequate writing skills. Further, more and more employers are declaring writing to be a "core competence for hiring and advancement."

"It shocks me how many people come out of schools—good schools—and can't write," says Linda Barrington, a research director and labor economist for a major think tank. "It drives me crazy."

Lorrie Foster, also a research director at the same organization, agrees. "Bosses are under such time pressure. If I have three people write a report and only one of them does it neatly and with proper style, then I know I don't have to work that hard with that person to get it ready for my boss. Yes, everyone should look for the diamond in the rough, but there are only twenty-four hours in a day, and we're already working 24/7. We just don't have the time to work with someone a lot."

In its report, the commission found that people who cannot write and communicate clearly "will not be hired, and if already working, are unlikely to last long enough to be considered for promotion."

Further, half of the 120 human resource executives polled by the group said they take writing into consideration when hiring professional employees and when making promotion decisions. "In most cases, writing ability could be your ticket in . . . or it could be your ticket out," said one respondent. Another noted: "You can't move up without writing skills."

The survey also found that two-thirds of salaried employees in large American companies have some writing responsibility. "All employees must have writing ability . . . manufacturing documentation, operating procedures, reporting problems, lab safety, waste-disposal operations—all have to be crystal clear," said one human resources director.

Finally, the commission estimated that remedying deficiencies in writing costs American corporations as much as $3.1 billion annually.

Just think of how your boss would sit up and take notice if you could prove you were a solid writer! Whether it was writing a couple of paragraphs on a customer complaint or finding errors in a report you review, the ability to write could definitely put a shine on your star.

If you know you need writing improvement (and everyone does no matter the skill level), here are some places to begin:

★ Read. It doesn't matter whether it's a newspaper, magazine or a book. The more you read, the more familiar you become with how sentences should be formed, proper spelling, grammar and paragraph structure.

★ Don't outsmart yourself. "Purification of unliquidated obligations is essential for the early identification and correction of invalid obligation amounts to ensure full and effective fund utilization," wrote a midlevel professional at a federal agency.[6] I have no idea what this means, and probably no one else does, either. An old rule of journalism is to keep

---

[6] Richard Lauchman, *Plain Style* (Amacom, 1993)

your writing clear enough that a twelve-year-old can understand it. Don't search for a bunch of big words to make you look smarter—writing clearly and concisely is more important. The quicker a boss can get the point you're trying to make, the better.

★ Work to improve. Someone once told me that it's easier to write badly than to write well, and I think that's very true. You must work at the writing craft—take a class or ask someone to help you. Many employers offer to pay for business writing or technical writing courses—jump at the chance if it's provided. More than 40 percent of the companies responding to the commission survey said they offer or require training for salaried employees with writing deficiencies.

★ Close your eyes. Kind of hard to write with your eyes shut, I know. But before you write, close your eyes and visualize what it is you want to say. Think of descriptive words that give more meaning to the reader. See the action you want to convey in your head: Did your coworkers *talk* about the contract or did they *debate* it? Was the customer *satisfied* or *ecstatic*?

★ Be concise. If a house was on fire, you wouldn't run to the fire department and say, "As I was perusing the neighborhood and its surrounding areas, I came upon a single-story structure with peeling paint that reminded me of one I lived in as a child with my family. This house, which really had some lovely lilacs near the front gate, appeared to have fire emerging from the windows . . ." No way! You would say, "There's a house on fire!" My point: Get to the point.

★ Avoid slang. "The inspectors for the job are ballers," won't mean much to anyone over the age of nineteen. Instead, write clearly: "The inspectors perform well."

★ Use correct names. Don't just guess at the spelling of a person's name or business. Always consult a phone book, professional directory or call the company to get correct information. One of my first journalism professors noted that Smith can also be spelled "Smithe" or "Smythe." It's always best to double-check.

★ Reread your work. Even though spell-check makes our lives easier, it's not perfect. Always proof your work several times—it often helps to walk away from it if you can and return to it hours or days later to give it another look. If you don't have that luxury, ask a coworker to read it.

★ Play word games. Crossword puzzles, anagrams, Scrabble and a host of other games and puzzles available online or in print form offer you a chance to grow your skills while having fun at the same time.

★ Take a class. Enroll in a creative writing class at a local college, or take a weekend seminar. Go to an author's symposium and listen to how the pros perfect their craft.

Another easy way to improve your writing and spelling is by using the Merriam-Webster online site at www.m-w.com, which includes a free, searchable dictionary and thesaurus, word games and vocabulary reference tools.

10. Failing to Write Thank-You Notes

As a child, your mom or your teacher probably taught you how to write thank-you notes. But if you haven't written one since the fifth grade, or your mom still writes them for you, then it's time you stopped avoiding the practice and learned the art of the business thank-you note.

"A handwritten thank-you note allows you to manage your own image and your own reputation," says Amy Dorn Kopelan, executive director of a coaching and training program for women in the early stages of their career. "Remember that your reputation is something that you own and no one can take away from you. You can stand out and be remembered or lost in the crowd."

Some basics of the business thank-you note:

* Pick up a pen and paper. While it's OK to send an e-mail or voice mail, a written thank-you note will have much greater impact. Use personal stationery or at least invest in some nice, blank cards. If you send e-mail, remember that it still is a written communication so you need to not only be professional, but follow the rules of grammar and spelling.

★ Keep it simple. Most thank-you notes need only a couple of basic ingredients: why you're writing the note and sincerity. Let someone know that the kindness made a difference. "Thank you for introducing me to your colleague, Joe Jones. I found him to be very helpful for my upcoming presentation and I can't wait to share his insights with others. I hope that I may be able to return the favor one day." Even if you're less than enthusiastic about a gift, you shouldn't let that stop you from sending a thank-you note: "Thank you for the bag of buffalo entrails. What an interesting and unique holiday gift. I appreciate you thinking of me."

★ Stop putting it off. Many of those who don't write thank-you notes claim they've waited too long to say thank you so they're embarrassed and just feel they should forget the whole thing. That only compounds the error. If you feel like it's really been a long time, say something like: "I've been remiss in not telling you sooner that I really enjoyed the conference. I learned so many important things I know I'll use in the coming year. I found your staff to be so helpful and I really appreciate it." Keep the focus on telling the person how much you value something and that your appreciation is sincere—no matter how late it is in coming.

★ Be prepared. If you know you'll be attending a conference or if holiday time is approaching, get your thank-you notes ready. Have enough notes on hand, along with stamped envelopes. If you dread writing the notes, at least have some with a thank-you message already inscribed inside. Some might consider this cheating but I say it's better than sending nothing at all.

Finally, learn from others. If you receive a thank-you note that is well done, keep it with your blank thank-you cards so that you can follow that example when writing one of your own.

11. Committing E-mail Blunders

Many of us now regard e-mail just like talking on the phone—quick and easy and a great way to take care of personal business. We send a reminder to our brother about Mom's birthday. We forward a political joke to twelve friends and we write to our significant other about a run-in with a coworker. Nothing obscene, right? What's the harm?

For companies, there is plenty of harm, and much of it is in lost productivity and legal issues. PC Delete says that more than 40 percent of bosses spy on employees to find out if you're surfing the Internet on company time. Xerox canned forty workers after they were nabbed for spending work hours shopping online, and one in five companies has fired workers over e-mail abuses.

Why such reactions? E-mail can be stored indefinitely on any computer, including your ex-boyfriend's hard drive. He can forward your message to any number of people, who can then copy it and send it along. So you're not just sending a message to a sister or a roommate, you're sending it to the world. And that is what they call "lawsuit heaven" in lawyer lingo.

Michael R. Overly, a lawyer specializing in information technology, says that e-mails have been the focus of dozens and dozens of lawsuits claiming everything from sexual harassment to defamation.[7]

He says a big problem is that many people treat e-mail "like a telephone conversation."

Electronic experts say that even if you delete your "sent" and "received" messages and empty the trash bin, there is software available that can revive these messages months after they were thought to be dead, and some companies even use "keystroke" monitoring that can monitor every letter you type. So, even if you don't fire off that angry memo, the boss can still find out about it. In fact, nearly 80 percent of major U.S. corporations electronically monitor their employees by checking their e-mail, Internet use, phone calls, computer files—or by videotaping them at work.[8]

It's important to note that the courts have consistently come down on the side of employers in cases of electronic monitoring on the job. So when using e-mail, you should always:

* Keep it strictly business. Don't try to be cute, funny, sarcastic or whimsical. Some companies have absolutely no sense of humor and e-mail is not the way to try to give them one.

* Think like a lawyer. You could get dragged into testifying in a legal matter if you even casually mention in e-mail a situation that has legal ramifications. Be careful what you put in writing.

[7] Michael R. Overly, *E-Policy: How to Develop Computer, E-mail, and Internet Guidelines to Protect Your Company and Its Assets* (Amacom, 1998)
[8] PC Delete, www.pcdelete.com/stats/htm

★ Think big. Just one employee using the company's system for illegal activity can result in the employer's entire computer system being seized by the government to preserve evidence. Wouldn't your boss think that was just peachy?

At the same time, misusing e-mail can result in litigation from other states or even other countries. Several courts have found that just sending the electronic message into their area gives them jurisdiction.

Overly says that to avoid getting into trouble, employees should make sure the content of all communications is accurate. Users should take the same care in drafting e-mail and other electronic documents as they would for any other written communication. Anything created on the computer may, and likely will, be reviewed by others.

While on the subject of e-mail, let me also address the most common e-mail blunders and how to correct them:

★ E-mails are forever. Use correct spelling and grammar in e-mail, and avoid using acronyms that not everyone may understand. Remember that e-mails can reflect not only your professionalism, but your intelligence and maturity. Focus on making sure your e-mails will stand the test of time— whether they are reviewed in six months or six years, they should be a positive reflection of you.

★ Stop spamming. Think carefully before you forward messages or information to others. Do they really need to see it, or do you just think it's "neat"? Maybe it's more appropriate to post it on the bulletin board and let people read it if they want instead of clogging up their e-mail.

★ Speak up. Don't use e-mail when you need to have a conversation—an e-mail will make the task too laborious. When you need to bounce ideas back and forth, an e-mail will not only be inefficient but possibly lead to a less favorable outcome—such as the reader hitting the "delete" button.

★ Structure messages properly. Study newspaper headlines for ideas on how best to communicate your message in the subject line. Use active words such as "cancel Jan. 15 meeting." In the first line of your message, indicate why you're sending it, such as a decision is needed or a request is being made. In journalistic terms, don't "bury the lead" by making the reader slog through a long introductory passage before stating what your key point is.

★ Think twice about "reply all." If you receive a congratulatory note, there's no need to reply "thanks" to everyone. Same with company news. Don't include everyone unless everyone needs to know. Always be careful when hitting the reply button. Sometimes you don't need to respond, and messages have more impact if the receivers don't feel you're always inundating them with useless information.

★ Let the reader off the hook. End a message with "no action required" or "all set." Better yet, "no reply necessary."

12. Failing to Speak Intelligently

Greg Ragland was an accounting auditor, confident in his ability to wrangle numbers. But then he discovered that his job wasn't just a lot of calculations—it was 90 percent descriptive, which meant that a lot of verbal and written communication was required. It wasn't long before Ragland's boss told him he had to improve those skills.

He recalls that he began listening carefully to the way his managers and coworkers communicated in meetings. He wrote down words they said frequently, noting the context in which the words were used. He began practicing words he heard that he liked, finding ways to incorporate them naturally into his everyday speech.

Ragland became such a word enthusiast that he turned it into a business, offering courses to those interested in improving their own speech. He says that the inability to speak well in the workplace is a growing problem that hurts careers.

"People are timid at work because they don't have the confidence in their vocabulary to speak up so they'll talk around something," he says. "If you have a limited vocabulary it can cause you to miss information and ideas from the higher-ups, because you can't keep up with them. It also causes you to read slower and affects your ability to write."

And it's not just the words you use, but the way you say them. Experts say that unless you enunciate clearly, use inflection in your voice and use pauses effectively, then others will lose interest in what you have to say—never a good thing at work. This is especially true when speaking to the boss. Bosses often are pushed for time and form quick impressions of a person in a short amount of time. If you mumble and stumble when speaking to the boss, searching for the right words or using some incorrectly, he may have a reason to avoid listening to you in the future. And once the boss stops giving redence to what you have to say, you're in trouble.

"You are judged by the way you speak. If you have poor grammar and say things incorrectly, then a judgment is going to be made about your professionalism and your skills," says Linda Barrington, a research director and labor economist for a major think tank.

It's never too late to improve your vocabulary and your ability to speak well. Some ways to improve your communication skills:

⋆ Focus on self-improvement. Do you say "acrossed" when you should say "across"? What about "chester drawers" instead of "chest of drawers"? What about "aks" instead of "ask"? (This mispronunciation has been around for more than 1,000 years according to linguists.) Do you bungle phrases by saying "for all intensive purposes" instead of "for all intents and purposes"?

The website www.yourdictionary.com offers the top 100 most mispronounced words and phrases in the English language. It's a great place to start getting a handle on your goofs. Another way to improve is to read more "highbrow" publications that correctly use phrases or words you may have been mangling.

Also, remember to use foreign words and phrases correctly. Don't use "ad infinitum" or "ad nauseam" or "joie de vivre" unless you know exactly how to say it and what it means. If needed, consult a high school or college language teacher for just the right pronunciation so you won't become persona non grata with the boss.

★ Know your power words. Listen carefully to the words frequently used by your boss and other executives. Ragland says some top "power" words include: acumen, affinity, ad hoc, ascertain, enumerate, pragmatic and visceral. He suggests writing such words in a notebook and describing how the word was used—the story behind the word. This helps you to later integrate the word into a similar situation.

★ Spot talent. If you know someone who has a way with words, try to spend time with him or her. Look for someone who has a varied vocabulary and seems to hold the interest of others easily. Engage this person in conversation to improve your own speaking skills. Or consider joining a book club—avid readers often have a varied and extensive vocabulary.

★ Get comfortable. You may often feel silly or unsure when incorporating a new word or phrase into your everyday speech. Practice the new word a couple of dozen times and instances where it might be used. Ragland says usually a word must be used three times before it becomes a permanent part of your speech.

⋆ Don't rush. Some of the most effective speakers make a strong statement—then pause—before continuing. This gives emphasis to what you say.

⋆ Get on your feet. Try to stand as much as you can when you speak to someone. This not only places you in a strong physical position, but it allows your voice to emerge clearly and sound more confident (this rule applies even when speaking on the phone). If you cannot stand, then sit up straight and face the other person.

⋆ Make eye contact. Don't look at the floor, your hands, your feet or even what is going on over the boss's shoulder when you're speaking to him. Look him in the eye and give him your complete attention—bosses want to feel that talking to them is the most important thing happening at that moment. Don't fidget, shift your feet or hide your hands. Those body signals divert attention away from your message.

⋆ Avoid slang. As I've mentioned before, slang can be confusing at best, and offensive at worst. Bosses may find "I'm gonna chill at my crib and I'll holla at you soon" not only confusing but irritating and immature.

13. Wearing the Wrong Thing to Work

If you want to break the ice at a cocktail party, just ask people what they think are appropriate clothes for work. The discussion will probably rage for an hour—dressing for work is something about which we all have an opinion.

Some folks will argue that no one should tell you what to wear—clothes are an individual expression and an individual right. Others will tell you that ties or dresses are stupid and wearing a pair of khakis and a T-shirt is just fine. Still others will say they're not quite sure about the particulars of appropriate dressing, but they know the wrong thing when they see it.

I remember when the "casual Friday" theme came into vogue years ago. A boss I was interviewing for a story told me he was deluged with questions about what was "casual" attire. He didn't know how to explain it clearly, and some employees began showing up for work in clothing more appropriate for a night at Studio 54 or for mowing the back forty. The boss, in frustration, went through a couple of magazines and ripped out photos of models wearing what he believed to be appropriate casual Friday attire and posted them on the employee bulletin board.

Unlike him, some bosses didn't take the initiative early on to define causal dress, hence the ratty jeans or microminis that popped up everywhere from banks to boardrooms. Many companies are now so aghast at what employees choose to wear to work that they're reinstituting dress codes.

"If you dress inappropriately, it creates a less-than-serious environment," says Lorrie Foster, a research director with a major think tank. "It's distracting."

It's important to understand that just because your boss hasn't clearly defined a dress code it doesn't mean he's blasé about what you wear. A boss definitely cares that you present an image that doesn't annoy coworkers or offend customers or—horrors!—embarrass him in front of his boss. Dressing incorrectly is irritating to the boss—your lime-green spandex miniskirt or grubby pants are easy to spot and bug him every time he lays eyes on you. Do you think the boss wants to send a poorly dressed employee to meet with important clients or to serve as a representative of the company? Not if he can help it.

You might not agree with clothing rules for work. Tough. After work, you can put on your muscle shirt and board shorts. Cut loose and be yourself. But as long as you're on the company's time and dime, there are some rules you need to follow:

★ Don't be too casual. Even if you have a "casual" work dress code, the problem with wearing clothes that are too baggy or too worn (and may resemble pajamas) is that they don't say to the boss, "I'm ready to work." Anything you would wear to sleep in or hang out with friends at home watching old movies is not appropriate for work.

★ No "clubbing" clothes. Supertight clothes or revealing shirts, skirts, pants or anything else you can wear to a bar are not appropriate for work. This also includes anything that shines, glitters, sparkles or glows in the dark.

★ No VPL. Please, no visible panty lines or shirts that clearly reveal your favorite Wonderbra. Hike up the britches so they're not exposing two inches of boxers, and do not wear only an undershirt. Get a full-length mirror and stand in good light so that you can check out the VPL and any other "don'ts" before leaving for work.

★ No advertising. It's been popular for some time now to wear T-shirts proclaiming everything from "I'm always right" to "Princess." The boss gets mighty uncomfortable with others staring at a female employee's chest, trying to read the shirt (a sexual harassment lawsuit in the making). Male employees wearing shirts with statements just look like they should be going to a frat party. Also, no T-shirts advertising bars, resorts or political candidates.

★ Don't reveal too much. The popularity of midriff-baring shirts has made the whole issue of showing skin even worse for bosses. Even if the shirt manages to meet the top of your pants when you are standing, it won't remain that way when you sit or move more than a fingernail at work. Either tuck your shirt in or make sure it's long enough to cover your midriff area when you move around. For women, it's also important that shirts are not too revealing with low-cut necklines or gaping armholes. Don't wear anything with spaghetti straps or a really short skirt or dress. No shorts for men or women.

★ Cover tattoos. OK, before someone suggests it, if you work in a tattoo parlor this doesn't apply. And there are probably other work environments where tattoos and piercings are de rigueur. If you're not sure, look at the boss and the boss's boss. If they're peppered with tattoos and look like human pincushions, go right ahead. But for everyone else: Cover the tattoos and limit the piercings. In a Vault.com survey of 500 readers, it was found that 42 percent of managers said they would lower their opinion of someone based on his or her tattoos or body piercings. Learn from one manager who wrote: "I did not reveal my tattoos until I was on a company awards outing in the mountains, by wearing shorts and a tank top. After that, it seemed that I was almost purposely excluded from outings. And they stopped using me as a trainer even though the guy they were using was not certified."

A good rule of thumb: Cover visible tattoos with clothing or makeup, and confine piercings to one in each ear while at work.

★ Use your head. Hair trends come and go. What is "in" this week will be "out" next week. But the one thing that doesn't change is the way hair is viewed at work. It shouldn't be a distraction. That means if it is colored by Kool-Aid, if it's dirty, messy or in an elaborate style not seen since Liz Taylor played Cleopatra, then it's not appropriate for work. Men should avoid the *Miami Vice* look and shave every day.

★ Check smells. This has become a greater issue as people are working in greater proximity than ever before. Many employees have professed allergies to heavy perfumes or colognes, so it's best to avoid them. And shower daily—every boss in the history of the universe has a story about having to tell a worker he or she has body odor. They all hate doing it.

★ Rules still apply when you're pregnant. This is a relatively new category that has to be addressed, mostly because it's become popular to bare the blooming belly or wear T-shirts that say something like "Sleeps Well with Others." Follow the same rules as everyone else even if you do have a little bundle of joy on the way. It's popular in the celebrity world to be more revealing when pregnant, but it's still not OK at work.

★ Remember that neatness counts. It's often the little things that trip up many workers. Always keep shoes shined and clean. Hems should be hemmed, not flapping loose or repaired with a stapler. Clothes don't have to be starched but they should not be wrinkled (and yes, you have to iron the front *and* the back). Even if you can't afford expensive clothes, you can always take the time to make sure your appearance looks neat.

Finally, remember that bosses are the most comfortable with others who are like them. That means if the boss lives in khakis and T-shirts, then that's probably OK for you. If, however, the boss never enters the office without a tie and jacket, with shoes shining and face freshly shaved, then you know that's your cue.

14. Behaving Immaturely at Company Parties

You know things are getting out of hand at office parties when employers spend more time worrying about lawsuits rather than if there's enough food and drink.

Get in a little car accident after the holiday office party and the other car has passengers who are injured? Your employer can be held liable for letting you drink and drive. Get a little too familiar with either your hands or your words with a coworker at the company picnic? You might just get slapped with a sexual harassment claim.

"A lot of people think that because it's a party, then the same rules that exist in the office do not apply," says Shannon Adcock, a lawyer specializing in labor and employment law. "But they do."

Which is why bosses care a lot about how you behave at a company party, whether it's an awards banquet, a picnic or a holiday bash. To bosses, you are still "at work." That means just as you wouldn't kiss a coworker at work, you shouldn't do it at the office party. Just as you wouldn't get sloshed at work, you should not do it at the company picnic.

Yet time and again employees seem to lose good sense at office parties. The office supply firm Quill found in a survey that "the most embarrassing" moments admitted by different coworkers while attending a work party included getting caught kissing the boss's son, flashing a boss while dancing too boisterously, falling on the dance floor and ripping a dress while doing the limbo.

What this should remind us all is that Monday always comes. In the harsh glare of office lights while standing around the water cooler, people naturally are going to discuss the party—and high on the list of favorite topics is "People Who Made Fools of Themselves at the Party." Maybe silly behavior will get a laugh or two. But you can bet reputations will be tarnished and probably none more so than the boss's.

"You are being interviewed and assessed 24/7, and that includes at office parties," says Amy Dorn Kopelan, executive director of a coaching and training program for women in the early stages of their career. "Whether you're at the golf course or in the ladies' room, you're always doing business and you're always being judged."

The thing to do before an office party is plan ahead and look at it as an opportunity to impress—not depress—the boss. You should:

★ Limit drinking. If you're driving, don't drink. If you go with someone, agree who will be the designated driver. If you don't want to answer questions about not imbibing, simply get a glass of tonic water with a lime. Add a straw and no one will know it's not a mixed drink. Don't think that just because spirits are provided it is an "all you can drink and still remain standing" affair.

★ Be social. It is a party after all. Don't corner the boss and begin discussing the latest problem at work. Use it as an opportunity to learn about others. Safe topics include hobbies,
sports and the weather. Don't hang out only with people
from your department. Walk up to someone and say, "Mary
Jones from purchasing" while offering a handshake. Most
people will immediately respond with their name and department. You don't have to have a long discussion—you
want to use the opportunity to make your name and face
more familiar to others. At the same time, being social does
not mean flirting, which often is the first step to a sexual harassment claim.

★ Keep your radar humming. Move away from groups where
the action is becoming a bit too lively. Groups that are too
loud, drinking too much, gossiping about work or drawing
attention in any way should be avoided. At the same time,
don't be caught with the "dead end" group. You know—the
ones who don't smile, don't laugh, don't talk and look as if
they'd rather be kicked down the stairs than be at the party.
Bosses can see this kind of behavior as rude and insulting,
especially since the company is footing the bill.

★ Be responsible for others. If you've brought a date, a spouse
or even a friend, then you are responsible for their behavior.
If a partner drinks too much it's time to get some hot coffee
or a breath of fresh air—and even claim a fake illness and go
home if you believe the person is really too inebriated to follow correct behavior. One of the biggest problems at company functions is friends or family members letting "slip"
what the employee really thinks of a boss or others. It's best

if you ask those attending with you to please avoid discussing your work—you never know who is listening.

★ Dress appropriately. Before any function, ask what the dress code will be. Holiday parties seem to trigger the need for some employees to resort to "clubbing" attire, which is inappropriate for any company event. Stick to conservative wear. As for picnics or more casual events, don't wear your oldest T-shirt and jeans, and always wear a swimsuit under a nontransparent cover-up when not in the water. You still want to appear neat and put together. If there are photos being taken, either put down your drink or lower it to your side while it's being taken. These kinds of photos often get posted at work—it looks better if you aren't caught for all eternity with a beer in your hand.

★ Use good manners. Always remember to find out who planned the party and personally thank them. Greet your boss when you arrive and make sure you say farewell or thank him as you leave if he was responsible in some way for the event. Introduce guests to others and don't dominate conversations. Don't gossip or whine about work—it's not the time or place and you'll be seen as a real bore. If you're going to eat, don't overdo it. Sample the buffet—don't inhale it. You can eat something before the event to take the edge off your appetite, or plan on going somewhere after the event to chow down.

One final note: No ditching the party. You may think it's easier to just blow it off, but attending an office party is important. It gives the boss a chance to see you outside the work environment, and it gives you an opportunity to meet others in a casual setting. The boss should feel that even when you're out of the work environment you are a pleasant, polite and professional person who deserves his confidence and respect.

So even if you go for just thirty minutes, shake some hands, share some laughs and call it a success. Just don't be the one shutting down the bar and dancing until the wee hours.

15. Being Disorganized

Dear Anita,
I have never been a super-neat person, but there is a method to my madness. I mean, if I have some time, I can find anything I need. But my coworkers kid me that I'm so disorganized I couldn't find my ass with both hands. The point is, I do my job and I do it well. I think they should just mind their own business. What can I say to them?
Fumin' Frank

Dear Frank,
If I were you, I'd tell those coworkers, "thank you." Bosses see a disorganized space and think: Disorganized work equals disorganized mind. Be grateful your coworkers pointed it out so that now you can clean it up. So, grab that Dumpster, Frank, and get busy!
Anita

No matter what kind of work you do, chances are you have some kind of workstation. A delivery driver has the inside of a truck or van, a store clerk has a cash register and a teacher has a desk.

Each of these spaces may have personal mementos, or a particular set of pens and papers, but each workspace usually bears the personal mark of the employee.

But for thousands of workers, that personal mark is one of chaos. Junk in the truck. Clutter at the cash register. Paper piles on the desk. All these spaces are different, yet very much the same: They all tell the boss that the employee has a problem. Why? Because in the boss's eyes, a worker who is unorganized and messy at work is probably not working at a high level of productivity and efficiency.

And while your personal landfill may be the butt of many jokes from coworkers, the boss isn't amused. All those "messiest desk" awards are fine when you're talking about your desk at home, but a space at work that could possibly be harboring flesh-eating bacteria isn't that cute to the boss.

A study of 2,611 employers by office supplies manufacturer Esselte found that more than half of the respondents said that an employee's level of organization is taken into account during annual reviews, and neater workers were more likely to be noticed, appreciated and promoted.

The problem of disorganization is nothing new and it is pretty pervasive. Why else would we have "get organized" days and/or months? There are even contests where the person with the messiest desk at work gets a free workspace makeover by organization experts.

But having a messy space at work isn't seen by the boss as funny or cute or endearing. It isn't seen as a sign that you are working hard. In fact, it may be seen as a sign that you're hardly working. A messy space annoys the boss because it tells her that you're not only working inefficiently but bugging everyone in the process.

Perhaps your clutter problem may be your way of controlling your space or reflects your inability to deal with separation issues. Maybe it's a vitamin deficiency or goes back to the fact that you didn't get a puppy as a child. Whatever. The point is that the boss doesn't care *why* you do it—she just wants you to *stop* doing it.

So go ahead and consult Dr. Phil on your deeper issues, but take time now to get yourself organized. You need to do the following:

★ Trim the paper. It's estimated that office workers use 200 sheets of paper a day. Dump unnecessary paper in the recycling bin. If you're receiving duplicates, trace it back to the source and ask for the problem to be corrected. If you're constantly being given unwanted reports, ask to be deleted from the list. Ask yourself, "What is the worst that can happen if I throw this away?"

★ File it. For many workers, "filing" means moving piles of paper from the desk to the floor. If your boss asks you for a certain piece of information, you should be able to put your hands on it quickly. The only way to do that is by filing it, not adding it to a disorganized pile. The boss will not appreciate having to cool her heels while you search through six levels of chaos for something she has requested.

★ Color it. A good rule of thumb is to have the files labeled or color-coded: red for action, blue for items that will be needed for future reference, green for anything financial and yellow for long-term projects. If you don't like this color combination, feel free to change it. The important thing is to use one that makes it easy for you to stay organized.

★ Use technology. Don't hold on to paper copies of reports that are already in your computer. Avoid printing out everything you receive. Instead, establish a filing system—even for e-mail—on your computer to keep everything on track. If you're not sure how to do that, ask someone with computer proficiency to help you. Ask others to stop forwarding you messages unless they affect you, and request to be removed from e-mail lists that do not help you do your job.

★ Organize for five minutes each day. Sharon Mann, an organizational expert with Esselte, says that by taking a few minutes at the end of your day you can put your space in order. Make sure things are in the right folder, unnecessary items are in the trash and the work you will need the next day is at hand. "You need to work every day in a way that shows others you are truly working. That means you should be able to know exactly where something is within ten seconds if it's a current project and within minutes if it's something you're not working on currently," she says.

Still, that may be easier said that done. Mann says that 37 percent of workers get anxious when deciding how to handle clutter. If you think you can't handle doing it all in one sitting, then spend a couple of minutes each day doing it until it's organized. Look at it as an ongoing project instead of a daily requirement.

★ Purge. Every six months, do a thorough cleaning of your space to make sure you aren't letting clutter creep in.

16. Being a Poor Listener

If you watch any cable television, it's commonplace to hear one person interrupt another, butting in rudely and shouting to be heard above someone else.

"I don't think you . . ."

"Just let me . . ."

"You're nothing but a . . ."

"Oh, yeah? Well, you . . ."

No one is listening to anyone else. And yet, it's typical of the way many people miscommunicate with each other in the workplace every day. It's estimated that while we spend 90 percent of our day communicating, we devote only 45 percent of that time to listening. Surveys show that 85 percent of Americans rate themselves as average or below in listening ability.

What that indicates is that—sooner or later—you're going to mess up because you weren't listening. And the odds are pretty good that the boss is going to be directly impacted by it.

Let's say, for example, that you don't pay much attention when a coworker tells you about past mistakes made with a customer. When you deal with the customer, you repeat those mistakes because you didn't listen and retain what the coworker said. The customer, understandably, is very angry because the mistakes have been repeated. He doesn't even bother yelling at you—he goes directly to your boss to complain. The boss investigates and finds out you were told of these problems, yet you obviously didn't listen or it wouldn't have happened again.

When asked by the boss why you didn't seem to get the message the first time, you think you have a perfect excuse: "Well, the phone was ringing," you tell the boss, "and that was right when birthday balloons were delivered to Chris. Plus, I think my mind was really on the fact that a snowstorm was predicted for late afternoon, not to mention I drank too much coffee and my stomach was upset."

While obviously a catalogue of some pretty diverse distractions, your excuse won't appease the boss. He will think that you should have (a) ignored the distractions and (b) listened better. He will begin to think of you as possibly undependable and unfocused. He will begin to watch you more closely, looking for other signs that you "don't have your listening ears on," as my son's preschool teacher used to say.

I know how difficult it can be to listen in today's world where phones, faxes, e-mails and pagers are always beeping or ringing. No one is willing to wait patiently—it seems everyone clamors for attention at once.

But you can put a stop to all the things that get you off track and decide that it's time you became a better listener. Try these strategies:

★ Take a deep breath. When someone at work begins talking to you, do you tense up, your mind immediately beginning to race with other thoughts?

Bill Lampton, a communications expert, says that while the average rate of speaking is 125 to 150 words a minute, our listening comprehension is about 400 to 500 words a minute. He says such a "listening gap" leaves room for our minds to roam. By taking a deep breath, you're saying to yourself, "Stop. Listen. Focus."

★ Don't interrupt. "It's the number one signal you're not paying attention," Lampton says. "It says that the other person's words are not as important as what you're going to say."

★ Don't finish anyone's sentences but your own. Unless you're clairvoyant, don't finish the thought of the person who's speaking. And even if sometimes you are just being enthusiastic when you jump in with, "I know just how you feel . . . ," or "I had the same thing happen . . . ," it is rude and shifts the focus from the speaker to you. You're supposed to be listening, not talking.

★ Don't fidget. Doodling on paper, playing with a pen, checking e-mail or flipping through mail when someone is speaking is not only rude, but guaranteed to distract you and prevent you from fully listening.

★ Blur the background. I remember an employee once told me one of the things she liked best about her CEO was that when she spoke to him, he totally ignored everything else going on around him while he listened to her. His undivided attention really made an impression on her. The lesson here is to blur the background so that your focus is completely on the speaker. Don't let your eyes shift around, and keep your body facing the other person.

★ Don't use selective hearing. If a coworker tells you: "I'll be happy to help you with that project if I can get approval from my direct supervisor," and all you hear is "I'll be happy to help," then you're only listening to part of the message. If you count on that help without knowing the outcome of the direct supervisor's decision, then you could be in a very deep creek without a paddle.

★ Summarize. After listening, summarize what you've just heard so that you're sure you didn't miss any pertinent points. "Let me make sure I've got this straight . . ." or "What you're saying is . . ." can clear up any communication confusion.

17. Losing Sleep

There is no worse feeling than lying awake, unable to sleep. Watching the clock's glowing numbers tick by: 2 a.m. . . . 3 a.m. . . . 4 a.m. . . . 5 a.m. And even if you finally do manage to doze off, it seems the alarm from hell is buzzing in your ear fifteen seconds after you fall asleep.

Sixty percent of adult Americans have sleep problems. Whether it's from stress (the number one cause of sleep problems, according to experts), jet lag or physical ailments, a majority of people are unable to fall asleep or stay asleep, or they sleep sporadically.

While the National Sleep Foundation (NSF) recommends seven to nine hours of sleep a night, their survey found that American adults average seven hours on weeknights, down about two hours a night over the last fifty years. Some twenty to thirty million adults experience occasional sleep problems, but forty million others suffer from one of the eighty-four identified sleep disorders.

The chronic lack of sleep is taking a toll on our bodies and our minds. The NSF has found sleep problems can make daily life more stressful and cause you to be less productive. It weakens your ability to concentrate to the point that accomplishing tasks becomes more difficult and you are more easily irritated. Overall, sleep loss has been found to affect tasks requiring memory, learning and logical reasoning.

Further, it's been determined that sleeplessness has been found to be a "significant predictor of absenteeism," says the NSF, and costs the national economy as much as $100 billion annually in lost productivity.

And, insufficient sleep can be very dangerous: The National Highway Traffic Safety Administration has estimated that more than 100,000 car crashes a year may be fatigue related, causing 1,500 deaths and tens of thousands of injuries annually.

So, it all comes down to this: If you're not getting enough sleep, you will be cranky, forgetful, less productive, more likely to call in sick and run the risk of having a wreck on the way to or from work. See why the boss cares if you're getting enough shut-eye?

Feeling Alert

While the boss can't tuck you into bed at night and make sure you're getting enough rest, she does expect you to find solutions to your sleep problems so that you can be at work, bright-eyed and bushy-tailed and ready to kick the competition's butt.

How do you know if you have a sleep problem? Experts say if it takes you more than thirty minutes to fall asleep, if you wake up frequently during the night or too early in the morning or have a hard time going back to sleep, then you may have a problem. Further, if you wake up feeling foggy and tired or are sleepy during the day, then you also need to seek some solutions to better sleep.

It's also important to remember that just because an average of eight hours of sleep a night is recommended, your sleep needs may be more or less. You may run at peak performance at six hours, while someone else may require ten hours. You should aim for enough quality sleep to feel alert during the day, even during monotonous situations.

Let me also point out that if you are a shift worker, or travel a great deal, you may be dealing with some special sleep problems. Twenty percent of U.S. employees are shift workers and biological rhythms can get thrown out of whack by such a work schedule. In fact, the NSF says that shift workers are two to five times more likely than employees with regular hours to fall asleep on the job.

If your sleep problems last more than a week, the NSF recommends that you visit with your doctor. Many of them will recommend lifestyle changes such as:

★ Cutting caffeine, nicotine and alcohol late in the afternoon and evening.

★ Avoiding napping during the day if you have trouble sleeping during at night.

★ Exercising regularly, but not closer than three hours before bedtime.

★ Establishing a relaxing, regular bedtime ritual such as turning lights down low and taking a hot bath.

★ Not using your bed for anything besides sex or sleep.

★ Making the sleep environment comfortable, quiet and dark.

★ Not tossing and turning if you can't fall asleep after thirty minutes. You should get back up and read or listen to soothing music until you feel sleepy.

Also, a friend who attended a sleep clinic told me that if I'm having trouble sleeping I should cover the numbers on my clocks. It seems that watching the numbers tick by only increases your anxiety when you can't sleep, which prevents you from dozing off. Sometimes it also helps to say, "I'm probably getting more sleep that I think I am," which also helps reduce your anxiety.

Making Adjustments

I know some people who swear by the "power nap." I once interviewed a top executive who said every afternoon about 3 p.m. he shut off his phone and took a nap either in his chair or on the floor of his office. He said it really recharged his batteries, and he no longer relied on coffee and sweets to keep him awake in the late afternoons—and that helped him sleep better at night.

While some cutting-edge companies have used "quiet rooms" for employees to catch some rest time, they're not widely available. Still, there is a chance that you could use some lunch hour or break time to rest quietly in your car or a lounge area, listening to quiet music or shutting your eyes and relaxing. Just don't forget to set some kind of timer to wake you in case you fall asleep, and never sleep more than thirty minutes or you could really screw up your nighttime rest.

For shift workers, the NSF says that naps throughout a shift are a good idea. My own dad was a shift worker for more than thirty years, and the man had developed the ability to nap anywhere, anytime. (I actually had to shake him awake five minutes before my wedding so that he could walk me down the aisle.)

The NSF says that shift workers should avoid long commutes and extended hours (shift workers are almost twice as likely to fall asleep driving home), work with others to help stay alert, remain active during breaks by shooting hoops or taking a walk, drink caffeinated beverages, do the most tedious tasks early in the shift (night-shift workers are most sleepy from 4 to 5 a.m.) and set up a support group with other shift workers to learn from one another on how to cope with sleep problems.

It's also recommended that as shift workers go home to sleep they wear dark glasses to block bright light, keep to the same bedtime and wake time schedule, even on weekends, and avoid using alcohol to sleep since tolerance will develop quickly and soon disturb sleep.

One of the growing sleep problems is with those workers who travel over different time zones. The NSF says that until recently, jet lag was not treated as a medical condition, but it is now included as one of the eighty-four known or suspected sleep disorders. It affects millions of people each year.

While people may have different jet lag symptoms, the severity is directly related to the number of time zones crossed by a flight and the symptoms typically last longer following an eastward flight. Those over age fifty are more likely to experience symptoms than those under age thirty. And if you're already experiencing sleep problems, there's a good chance that jet lag will be intensified.

If you know you're going to travel across time zones, then shift your sleep time a few days before traveling. If you're westbound, go to bed and wake up one hour later each day. Before going east, go to bed and wake up one hour earlier each day.

Whenever you travel, avoid alcohol and caffeine at least three to six hours before bedtime, and avoid heavy exercise close to bedtime. Use earplugs and blindfolds to reduce noise and light while sleeping.

The key to solving sleep problems is to take action right away to solve your dilemma, either through some self-help steps or through professional advice. A good night's rest should be a priority not only because it's a safety issue for you and others but because your health—and your job—depend on it.

18. Using Your Personal Cell Phone Too Much

Everyone loves to tell the stories of the "idiot" they've witnessed yakking on a cell phone at inappropriate times. The guy talking on his phone at a funeral. The woman driving ninety miles per hour, speaking into her phone while putting on lipstick, writing in a notebook and drinking coffee.

We can't believe it, we tell ourselves. What a moron! What a fool! We are so astounded by such idiotic behavior, in fact, that we simply must pick up our own personal cell phone at work to call our friends and family to tell them about it.

"Egads!" the friends and family agree. "What an idiot! What was this person thinking?"

The better question might be: What are *you* thinking? You're on *your* cell phone at *work*!

Most bosses don't mind when you use your personal cell phone to call and check on the kids after school, or let your friend know you're going to be late for dinner. Bosses are not ogres—they know that you have a personal life, and using a personal cell phone is not completely forbidden.

But have you ever considered that every time the boss sees you with that cell phone to your ear, he knows without a doubt that you are taking care of personal business? And when you're taking care of *personal* business, then that means you're not taking care of *business* business? You might as well run a sign up the flagpole that says, "Closed. Will return when I feel good and ready."

Bosses already feel employees spend too much time on personal business. A national poll by Accountemps of 150 senior executives in the nation's 1,000 largest companies reports that bosses say employees on average spend fifty-six minutes each day on nonbusiness-related e-mail, instant messaging and Internet use. Do you honestly think he's going to like seeing you gab on your cell phone as well?

At the same time, more bosses are becoming concerned about what employees might be doing with cell phones at work besides just talking. The increasingly sophisticated technological wonders of cell phones can allow anyone to photograph or download privileged or confidential information, such as customer lists and trade secrets.

And consider how coworkers feel about your cell phone addiction. If the boss can tell when you're conducting personal business, then it's also clear to others who may resent the way you're shirking your duties in order to tell a friend all about last night's date or discuss what the doctor said about your bunions.

"I think we feel we're just tethered to the things [cell phones]," says Dana May Casperson, a business etiquette expert. "Personally, I am offended hearing someone else's conversation."

That brings up another good point: People have a tendency to speak louder on cell phones, so anything you say might not just be heard by someone nearby, but by someone clear across the room. (Most people probably don't want to know about your bunions.)

Casperson says that most people are just "not aware" of how their behavior is not only a bad reflection on them personally but on the employer they represent as well.

"This isn't rocket science," she says. "But people just aren't thinking through what they are doing."

So, boys and girls, let's put on our thinking caps and consider the dos and don'ts of cell phone behavior as it relates to work:

* Turn. It. Off. Who doesn't love the "hang up and drive" bumper stickers? The same thing can be said of other situations. Why do you need your phone on during business meetings or meals? The world will not come to an end for an hour or two if your phone is turned off. I find it annoying to have someone put his phone on vibrate and then check it every time it does its thing. It's different, of course, if you're waiting for a kidney and don't want to be out of touch. In that case, just inform others that you are awaiting such a call. They will understand and appreciate your honesty. Also, keep the ring tone professional—"Let's Get Down Tonight" is not appropriate for the workplace.

* Set a time limit. If you get a personal call, watch your minutes. Any call that's going to take longer than five minutes should be returned either on break time or when you get home. This is especially true if the call is of a private nature because, seriously, your coworkers don't want to hear the details of your wart removal. As I mentioned, people tend to talk loudly on

cell phones ("cell yell") so chances are your entire department may become privy to your personal business.

★ Establish some rules. Let your mother and your best friend and your significant other know that you prefer not to be called at work unless the house is burning down or you've won the lottery. You may have to remind them when they call that you can't talk and will phone them back after work. Be sure you add that they should not resort to your work e-mail in order to communicate.

★ Be wise. I find it fascinating to watch people in airports and train stations and hotel lobbies gab away on their cell phones about business, talking about the deal they just made, who they talked with, what this means to the company, etc. I doubt the boss would appreciate it. Not only does it drive everyone around you nuts (except for me, a terrible eavesdropper) as you blab loudly about company business, but you never know who is listening and what they are learning because you don't have the sense to find a quiet corner. All businesses are highly competitive, and bosses don't appreciate you giving away information to everyone in Penn Station.

★ Put safety first. If you cause a traffic accident while talking on a cell phone and conducting company business, your company could be held legally liable. It's a good idea to pull over and finish a call rather than having the next one being placed to your boss, saying, "I just had an accident . . ."

19. Acting Like a Boor at Business Meals

Dear Anita,

I was at a business dinner with my boss and some clients and during the entire meal, I could feel my boss watching me. Since then, she hasn't asked me to attend any more business dinners. I'm kind of wondering if she was upset when I belched pretty loudly after the meal. But what was I supposed to do? It's not healthy to hold it in!

No Excuses

Dear No Excuses,

Was this gaseous incident before or after you stuck your gum on the side of the plate or picked your teeth with the wine list? Business meals are just that—business. If your table manners aren't a good reflection on your boss and your company, then yes, you're going to be left out. Now, wipe your chin.

Anita

I once attended a business lunch where the woman sitting across the table from me attacked her meal like it might try to crawl off her plate. Gripping the knife and fork as if they were weapons, her elbows sticking out sharply at ninety-degree angles, she went after her roast beef and green beans like a warrior princess.

The sounds emitted during this skirmish reminded me of the time my dog found a rabbit hole and stuck her snout in it, rooting and growling and gnashing her teeth.

Of course, the energy expended by this woman during her meal was bound to get messy—good thing she had the forethought to stick her napkin in her collar.

When she was done, a slight mist of sweat on her upper lip, she leaned back and wiped her chin. We realized she was done when she tossed her napkin on the table.

The rest of us, who had been frozen in a sort of horrified fascination as we watched her eat, simply muttered and tried to resume our meals. (Personally, I had lost my appetite. Must have been that vision of my dog going after that poor rabbit.)

Did this woman realize that her manners were less than desirable? I think not. I think she probably was just never taught the proper etiquette, or at least no one ever said anything to her about her manners. And that may be the case with your boss. It's not likely that she will tell you your manners are lacking. But you probably won't be invited to dine with her again, and she'll restrict your eating interactions with clients or others in the company.

In fact, more companies are sending employees to "etiquette lessons" after witnessing poor table manners or other rude habits. But if you'd rather take care of your own etiquette issues before being directed to such a class, don't wait—these skills are not something you want to just sort of "pick up" while watching others.

Good manners need to feel natural to you so that when a business meal takes place you can concentrate on business, not on which fork to use.

What are some key rules you need to know? Experts recommend you need to do the following:

★ Practice your manners. At home, eat in front of a mirror or even videotape a typical meal. Do you sit up straight? Put one hand in your lap? Use your napkin? Talk with your mouth full (a major pet peeve of many managers)? If you're used to eating on the coffee table while sitting on the floor in front of the television, begin eating at a proper dining table with all the required utensils so that you feel comfortable with the process.

* Plan ahead on what to eat. At a restaurant, don't order messy foods like spaghetti or nachos. Order something that you feel comfortable eating and have eaten before. If you're unfamiliar with the food, ask the waiter for a recommendation—you can usually get a description of the dish to help you make a decision. If the food arrives and you don't care for it, keep quiet and just sort of push it around your plate until others are done.

★ Be considerate of others. Let guests order first and don't order the most expensive thing on the menu. Be polite to the waiter—your rudeness to waitstaff is a signal to others that you're quite the jerk.

★ Watch the alcohol intake. Keep your liquor or wine consumption to a minimum. It's OK to order a nonalcoholic drink, but don't be the only one to order beer or alcohol.

★ Make the right moves. When you sit at the table, unfold your napkin and place it in your lap once everyone is seated. If you have to leave the table for any reason, put the napkin in your seat. When you are finished, your napkin should be placed to the left of your plate.

★ Keep track of the forks, forks, forks. It can be intimidating to face a plate surrounded by more than one fork. The rule is to use the fork farthest from the plate first. If you mess up, don't worry about it. Chances are, no one will notice unless you start juggling cutlery to correct the mistake. If you drop a utensil, don't pick it up, but let the waiter take care of it. Do not hold your fork as if it's a shovel.

★ Understand spoons. When using a spoon for soup, dip it away from you, moving from the front of the bowl to the back. Don't slurp. When you're done, leave the spoon on the plate underneath, not in the bowl.

★ Use the right place setting. Your bread plate is to the left of your dinner plate and your drink or coffee cup is to the right. Always pour a bottled beverage into a glass.

★ Wait to begin eating until everyone is served. In a restaurant, sometimes not all the food is delivered in one trip, so wait until everyone has a plate. If you go through a buffet line and return to your table ahead of others, wait for everyone to return before eating.

★ Take small bites. Tear off small portions of bread, butter each piece (with butter you have placed on your bread plate) and don't cram your mouth full. All bites of food should be kept small. If you look like a squirrel storing nuts in your cheeks, then you know portions are too large.

⋆ Don't lean. Keep elbows off the table until the meal is over.

⋆ Avoid picking and primping. If you get something caught in your teeth, swish water around (discreetly) in your mouth, or place your hand over your mouth while you (quickly) dislodge it. If you need to reapply lipstick, brush your hair, etc., do it in the restroom.

⋆ Remain attentive. Don't get so caught up in eating that you forget why you are there: to present a charming and professional persona to your boss or others. If business discussions are tabled for a while, ask questions about another person's interests, but stay away from sex, politics and religion.

Part Three

Snippy, Snotty and Socially Stunted:
Bosses Don't Give Great Projects to Those Who Can't Play Nice and Get Along with Others

It's been said that you can choose your friends but not your family. The same can be said of coworkers. When you take a job, you don't say to the boss, "OK, I'll work with Jane, but not with Fred—I just don't like him much."

While it's true that many fast friendships have been formed on the job, it's also true that workers have come to physical blows on the job because they drive one another batty. It's not pleasant to work with people you don't really like when you already have to put up with plagues, pollution, traffic jams and sugar-free chocolate.

Part of the problem is that we're physically forced to work closer than ever before. Organizations that are "flattening out" now have workers nearer one another to facilitate teamwork. Companies looking to trim increasing real estate costs have cut space, also forcing workers to be in tighter quarters.

And while bosses care about workers getting along with one another, they put together teams of employees based on the best use of skills and abilities—not whether they can be the best of friends. They know Jamie is a great accountant and Bobby is a great salesperson. If Bobby and Jamie don't necessarily want to be pals, that's fine with the boss. She just wants them to do their job and cooperate enough to get done what needs to get done.

It truly bugs a boss when she's got to referee employees like she's a playground supervisor. After all, she assumes that when she hires adults, they will act like adults. Being ugly to one another is not an option in her book. Anyone who forces her to take time away from her duties to deal with such immature matters as name-calling, snottiness, gossiping and rudeness will be seen as immature and unprofessional—attributes that don't get a person the plum assignments.

Whether you like it or not, the world of work is very diverse and getting more so every day. Outside of work, you may hang out with people who are pretty much like you, but that's not an option on the job. At work, you're going to be exposed to people of different nationalities, religions, genders, physical abilities and backgrounds. They may have different values and habits and goals, but they have one thing in common with you: They work for a living.

The boss figures that if you don't get that by now and if you can't control hurtful actions or words, then she can't take the chance of giving you assignments where you need to work well with others. And let's face it: No job is an island. No job stands alone. (My apologies to John Donne.)

Bosses don't want to face discrimination lawsuits because you are intolerant of others and they don't want to be embarrassed in front of their boss because you are a small-minded gossip. They don't want to have to keep running interference with other employees because you can't get along with a pomegranate.

So, be obnoxious, antisocial and demeaning on your own time. At work, bosses expect you to get along and play well with others.

20. Not Appreciating Coworkers

Dear Anita,

I am having trouble understanding why my boss tolerates some people I work with. These people are what I would call "perimeter" employees. You know the kind: They don't really contribute to the bottom line. They don't handle clients, they don't bring in business, and personally, I wonder what they do all day. I think their jobs could be outsourced, but I'm not sure how to suggest this to my boss. The money we save could be put to better use after all!

Hustlin' Harry

Dear Harry,

While a car can certainly run with only an engine, it sure isn't going anywhere without wheels. While you may be the engine, those people around you are the wheels. It's time you realized that all "parts" must work together for a business to be successful and move forward. If you can't get that, you may just wind up being roadkill.

Anita

There's a reason that actors thank anyone they've "ever met" when they receive an Oscar award. They know, as do many other highly successful people, that no one can do a job alone. On the job it often takes a cast of hundreds to bring off one important project—from the salesperson making the pitch to a client to the executive assistant who does research to the intern who works late to make sure all the files are labeled correctly.

Further, whether it's in a hot start-up company or in a Fortune 100 corporation, you can bet that sometime during your work life you're going to run across certain characters. Maybe you see them as "perimeter" employees, but that's a costly mistake. Without them, you're going to be fighting an uphill battle at work, possibly making the same mistakes over and over, or costing others valuable time and effort. Bosses know how important certain employees are, and they'll usually find a way to ease out the person who just doesn't get it.

So, let's start by forgetting for a moment the CEO, CFO and COO. Let's talk about Dr. No.

This Dr. No in the workplace is not the mad scientist of James Bond films, but the man or woman who knows everything there is to know about technology. This person can *feel* what's wrong with your motherboard, understands why your e-mail won't send and why your website is now in French. This person also knows, without you saying a word, that you have actually *whacked* a computer in frustration. Something he or she would never, never do.

My first real encounter with a Dr. No at work came when a gentleman of indeterminate age and clad in a brown lab coat answered my summons for computer help. (I have to admit I wondered about the lab coat, but I was afraid to ask and he certainly wasn't telling.)

I had begun to relate my troubles with the computer, when he began shaking his head in small, jerky movements, muttering under his breath. He never made eye contact, but slowly nudged me away from my chair and the computer monitor. His fingers gently rested on the keyboard. (I swear I heard a sigh come from the direction of the monitor, as if a child had just been stroked by a parent's loving hand.) With some gentle tapping and more muttering, Dr. No stepped away from my desk.

He left. I looked at my computer, and could see the ailment had been fixed. Dr. No had offered no explanation of what happened. He had tended his patient, and left.

Coworkers looked on, many grinning. When I asked what had just happened, a coworker laughed and said, "That was Dr. No. Get used to it."

Over the years in jobs with various companies, there was always a Dr. No. He didn't always wear a lab coat. Sometimes it was a guy with shaggy hair and beard who could have passed for Jeremiah Johnson. Or, it was a neatly buttoned-down female who could have been selling Avon door-to-door. But they all were very smart, very capable IT (information technology) people.

No matter their outward appearance, I knew that my life would be difficult without them. (I still remember the time my computer seized up after I spilled an entire cup of soda on a keyboard. The IT person took it away, bringing me another one. He never said a word to chastise me, although I certainly deserved it.)

What exactly makes these techies tick and how can we mere mortals get along with them?

Stan Gibson, executive editor of a major IT publication, says that most of us don't take the time to understand that these people are, well, *people*.

"They're not wizards," Gibson says. "No one understands everything. Sometimes there are unexplained behaviors of computers."

That means when you're stuck in cyber hell for some reason, don't blame the IT person. It could be that you let a virus into your midst when you opened that e-mail attachment from an unknown source—something IT departments warn against all the time. (And many workers ignore all the time.)

So, to begin establishing a good relationship with IT workers, you should try the following:

★ Educate yourself about their job. In this day and age, it sounds idiotic to say, "I don't understand computers or anything about them." That's like saying you can't get the grasp of how to use a telephone. Ask questions of the IT people about what you're doing wrong and how you can correct it. Take notes. Ask them about basic troubleshooting you can do yourself, instead of picking up the phone and whining to them every time there's a glitch.

★ Include them in the process. If you're working on a project that is going to require something special with a system, get their input from the first day. They want to be thought of as "strategic" in business planning. Or, let them in on your daily activities and get suggestions on how to be more efficient with your system use. There are new things happening every day, and these people make it their business to know.

★ Treat your computer with respect. No smacking the monitor, no pounding the keyboard in frustration. IT workers usually have a background in engineering, so it goes against their nature to do anything they consider risky—they'd rather take a system away from you than have it abused.

★ Avoid blaming them for frustrations. It doesn't help anyone to have you cast aspersions on IT people and their ability to handle problems. "Just like anyone else, they don't like failure associated with them personally," Gibson says.

Now let's discuss the polar opposite of Dr. No. One of the other prevalent characters—and often the most outgoing in any office—is Mom. Mom can be male or female and of any age, but all have one thing in common: The office couldn't run without them. I know we all like to think that our workplace couldn't run without us, but truly, if Mom is gone, the place goes to hell in a handbasket in no time.

That's because Mom holds the keys to the kingdom. She knows how to file health forms and which ones to fill out. She has a veritable Wal-Mart hidden in her desk: stain remover, aspirin, antacid, Band-Aids, cookies and a bicycle pump. She can give you the lowdown on nearly every person who has worked in the office, visits the office or is in the office next door. She can give you the best parking space, knows how to override the copier's code and has a key to the boss's office. She will be the best wingman you ever had if you treat her right. If you don't, you might as well put your foot in the shredder.

I discovered the office mom early in my working life, and quickly caught on to her place in the universe (the center), so I watched my step, careful to follow her dos and don'ts.

But others had to learn the hard way. Take, for example, one former coworker who had a bit of a prima donna complex. Filled with her own sense of self-importance, she walked up to Mom, who was having a conversation with another person. Instead of waiting politely for an opening, she interrupted, stating that she needed Mom to make airline reservations right away for a business trip.

In this case, Mom was a thirty-something man. He looked at the coworker and I knew from the look on his face that things were about to get very interesting. But my coworker was oblivious. Without an apology for the interruption, she again stated her demand—and definitely without a "please" or "thank you."

Big mistake.

Mom made the airline reservations from Washington, D.C., to New York all right—but it was via Houston.

The key to understanding and dealing with office moms is to realize they're not unlike your real-life mom. These people are caretakers—it's in their nature to help you fight a parking ticket or give you a great pumpkin bread recipe. But they face a world that doesn't necessarily appreciate them for all the little things they do that make things run smoothly. They are not the top wage earners, or the "stars" of the office, so they often may be overlooked in the daily scheme of things.

It cannot be stressed enough, however, that while they may not actively seek to do you harm if you dis them, it's not beyond them to make you pay for transgressions. Maybe your new desk chair doesn't get ordered or your time sheet gets misplaced. The point is that you've got to take care of Mom and she (or he) will take care of you.

What keeps Mom happy?

★ Always say "please" and "thank you," even if you only asked where to find more paper clips. Nothing is too trivial to ignore civility in Mom's book.

★ Show appreciation. This doesn't have to be too elaborate, but if you're going for a cup of coffee one day, ask Mom if she'd like something. This demonstrates that you're not overlooking her in your busy climb up the corporate ladder. Try to do this at least once a week.

★ Compliments are always welcome. Mom can spot bs, but that doesn't mean she doesn't appreciate sincere kudos: "Thanks for your help with that health form. I know you saved me hours of work." "That was a terrific cake you picked out for the office party. You have good taste!" "I noticed you cleaned out the coffeepot. It was really nice of you to do that since everyone uses it." Try this a couple of times a week.

★ Learn to apologize. While you're learning the rules of Mom's universe, you may slip up now and again. If you get it wrong, apologize immediately. Mom will forgive because she knows—*sigh!*—her job is never done.

That brings us to Oscar—as in Oscar the Grouch. You know, the old guy who sits in the corner, who has been there since the dawn of man and seems to periodically sleep with his eyes open. He can use a computer, but laments the loss of typewriters. He opens and reads his mail during office meetings.

Here's what many people fail to appreciate about Oscar: He is the history of the company. He knows things that no one else knows. He remembers the mistakes, the successes and the people who have walked in and out over the years. He knows what worked and what didn't. And yet, many people think him *ancient* history, so they don't bother to look deeper.

Hamilton Beazley has researched the role of long-term employees and says their importance to the success of a company—and its workers—cannot be overlooked.[9]

"You have to keep in mind that today to remain competitive, you must be a learning organization, not a forgetting organization," Beazley says.

That means that what Oscar knows is golden—so priceless in fact, that you'd be a fool not to learn everything you can from him. Remember, it's more than his knowledge of where the old files are kept—it's the emotional intelligence he has about the company and the people who have been in it.

To benefit from Oscar, you need to keep the following in mind:

★ Be respectful. Just for sheer perseverance, the long-term employee deserves respect. He has survived good times and bad. It's those hills and valleys of experience that make him so valuable. It's not always the superstars of the workplace who are the greatest asset—but the employee who puts one foot in front of the other every day, no matter what the situation.

★ Start slowly. Begin by getting to know Oscar in small ways. He may be standoffish at first, thinking you're just someone who is passing through. Ask him when he started for the company and who he worked with. Build from there, asking him about projects he worked on and what he considers the company's greatest achievements—and failures.

[9] Hamilton Beazley, Jeremiah Boenisch and David Harden, *Continuity Management* (Wiley, 2002)

★ Don't just dig dirt. You're not out to get the lowdown on everyone who walked through the place, but rather a sense of how various people and projects are interconnected. Try to get Oscar to put things into perspective—how the company responded to events going on at the time.

★ Keep it to yourself. Unless Oscar gives you the go-ahead, you shouldn't be sharing his memories with anyone else. While his remembrances of business past are important, he should be comfortable talking about them. Always ask permission to tell others.

★ Don't wait. Beazley says that when an employee walks out the door, "it's an asset giveaway." Since it's estimated that in 2010, someone will turn sixty-five every seven seconds, it's clear that older employees who leave with a vast store of knowledge will leave a world of hurt—and ignorance— behind them.

21. Failing to Delegate

See if this sounds familiar: You have reached a certain level of proficiency on the job. You know all the ins and outs, you know all the problems before they happen, you can predict most outcomes and explaining this to anyone else is just more trouble than it is worth. And, you would rather just take care of a task yourself and know it's being done right than risk asking someone to help who would then (probably) royally screw it up.

But then stuff starts to happen. You get talked into joining a new project or you volunteer for something. Before you know it, you're doing enough work to keep five people busy, let alone one person. But still you won't let go. Whether it's your own ego or some sick sense of control ("I may not be able to control many things in my life, but I can control this work"), not being able to delegate has a ripple effect.

This is when bosses get concerned. The boss comes to realize that you are trying to do too much without asking for help. He begins to worry that some things are going to get lost in the blizzard of work, that you're hoarding jobs that others should be doing. He wonders why you can't ask someone else to help you—do you have a problem with other people? Do coworkers dislike you and not want to help? Are mistakes going to be made because the work is not being done as efficiently as possible?

You may feel the boss doesn't care about how hard you work as long as the job gets done. But he's going to care when you crash—and that will happen, I guarantee it. It may not happen today or tomorrow, but failing to delegate will catch up with you sometime, possibly through sloppy mistakes or bottlenecks caused by your inefficient use of time.

And when it all sort of implodes, when the dozens of plates you have spinning in the air come crashing down, then you don't just have a problem—your boss has a problem. You waited too late to delegate so now he must stop what he's doing and find ways to divvy up the workload better—something you should have handled. The boss understands—even if you don't—that anyone who wants to move up the career ladder must know how to delegate effectively. Perhaps you aren't ready for more challenging assignments, he may surmise, if you can't handle your workload properly.

Richard Lamond, senior vice president and chief human resources officer of a national staffing company, says that those who want to be in the management ranks someday must know "that you get things done through others."

"Low performance is not tolerated, and that means that you've got to get other people involved when you want something accomplished," Lamond says.

At the same time, it's important that you understand what delegating is, and is not.

Delegating is not dumping the work you don't like onto someone else just to get rid of it. It is not asking someone else to help you with no explanation or follow-up or support.

It is, however, a chance for you to do the work that best grows your skills and abilities while helping someone else do the same. If done correctly, delegating not only helps your career, but others as well. And that is exactly the kind of delegation the boss wants.

The art of delegation means you need to:

★ Target the right person. "It's better not to delegate if you're going to give it to the wrong person," says Gene Griessman, a time management expert. "Because either it's not going to get done, or it's going to get done incorrectly. And you will have damaged your relationship with that person." That means you don't give a critically important task to someone you've never asked before, or ask a nontechnical person to deal with glitches in the computer system. Look for people who have demonstrated responsibility in the past or have skills that are needed for the job, such as organization or decision-making. Ask the person to take on a job that will interest him, and explain how doing the tasks can add to his skills and make him more valuable to the organization. Be upbeat and don't belittle the job. Saying, "This is such a no-brainer; anyone could do it," doesn't exactly make people jump at the chance.

★ Be supportive of the effort. Every person brings unique abilities and insight to a task. You must understand that if you ask someone for help, he isn't going to do the job exactly like you, but that doesn't make it wrong. Be appreciative of the fresh perspective being brought to the job. You need to be available for concerns or questions once you delegate a job—it's not fair if you aren't willing to provide support during the learning phase. At the same time, you need to back off and put your faith in the other person's ability to get the job done. While it's tempting to take a project back when mistakes are made, you've got to be willing to let the other person work out the minor kinks and realize that it's part of learning. That doesn't mean you don't step in if it's sinking faster than the *Titanic*, it just means that you don't hover and drive someone so nuts he never wants to help you again.

★ Set clear goals and deadlines. "This needs to be done by September 1. It's an important piece of the merger we are working on" tells the person not only when it's due but that the task is important for everyone's success. If this is the first time you've delegated to this person, you should check in periodically to make sure it's staying on track.

★ Keep communication open. If you delegate a task, let others know. "I've turned that part of the project over to Dan, so please direct your questions or concerns to him," you say. It doesn't make much sense to delegate, then spend all your time redirecting people. An e-mail or meeting announcement should cover the bases.

22. Being Intolerant

As a workplace journalist, I'm bombarded regularly with surveys of all kinds, ranging from what is the best kind of coffee to serve in the workplace to whether anyone really wants to work for Martha Stewart. But one day a particular survey caught my eye. It stated that the "incidence of ethnic and racial insults and other inappropriate remarks showed no decline in the workplace last year."[10]

The reason I was so interested in this finding was because I had been receiving some rather disturbing letters from readers of my workplace column. These letters, like many I receive, outlined a particular problem in the workplace. What was different, however, was that in each case the writer not only blamed a certain person for the trouble—but also the person's gender or the ethnic or religious group to which the person belonged.

I was surprised by the anger and resentment in those letters, but really taken aback by the ignorance and intolerance being ex-

[10] Novations/J. Howard & Associates, Boston, Mass.

pressed. With all the diverse faces in the workplace these days, I thought, were we actually moving backward, not forward, in our understanding and acceptance? How could anyone make such sweeping generalizations about people based on their interactions with one person?

I asked Rosalyn Taylor O'Neale, a diversity expert, her opinion.

"In the beginning, diversity was relatively simple," she says. "We had men learning to accept women in the workplace. Then later, it was whites learning to accept African-Americans. It all made pretty good sense—it was Americans accepting other Americans that they were used to being around."

Then, says O'Neale, the workplace diversity issues became more complex as gays, immigrants and the disabled began seeking "inclusivity."

At the same time, companies began operating "leaner and meaner" and workers worried about job security and future pay raises, she says.

"That's when people started looking for someone to blame," she says. "And they said, 'It's not *me*—it's *them*. The reason I'm not getting more is because of *those* people.'"

O'Neale adds that because most people hang out with someone like them in their private lives, it can be disconcerting to be exposed to different people in the workplace.

Still, she points out that workers must realize that "talent comes in all kinds of packages," and that a diverse team reaps all kinds of advantages. "Look at Dennis Rodman and Michael Jordan," she says. "They were different, but made a heck of a team."

Another reason workers must be more accommodating of everyone is because it's the law: Title VII of the Civil Rights Act of 1964 prohibits employment discrimination based on race, color, religion, sex or national origin. (For more information on the law, check out the Equal Employment Opportunity Commission website at www.eeoc.gov.)

"Companies not only don't want the negative publicity of a discrimination lawsuit but any such lawsuit is a direct reflection on the boss," O'Neale says. "A boss's success is based on a smooth-running team, and a lawsuit doesn't say that."

In order to survive these days, a company must be internationally competitive—no company operates in a vaccum regardless of the size or location. Bosses understand that their success depends on employees constantly generating new and creative solutions. If employees are intolerant of one another, that not only slows down the efficiency of the process but puts critical advances in jeopardy.

"Almost all bosses have seen at least one example of someone who came up with a great idea because they have different hobbies or interests," O'Neale says. "That's why diversity matters."

While the letters I mentioned earlier from readers expressed obvious bias, there are still many in the workplace who are not even aware that their actions or words are intolerant, discriminatory or hurtful. Could you be hostile or unaccomodating to others in the workplace because they are different than you? Is it possible you may be a "closet bigot," using excuses to avoid working cooperatively with diverse coworkers?

You need to keep the following in mind:

★ Be more aware of what you say. Often, what we consider the most casual or offhand comments are really insensitive to others. Have you ever said that someone is a "real slave driver"? To someone who is African-American, this comment may be offensive. Try to weed out such descriptions and instead say that someone is a "real taskmaster." You may be kidding when you claim that "all women are gossips" but that is inappropriate to the females in the workplace, just as someone saying "all men are lazy slobs" is unfair. Anything that has a "those people" kind of edge to it should be omitted from your language in the workplace.

* Speak up if there's a problem. If you find something a coworker says is insensitive, take the person aside and calmly say, "You know, you're giving all women a bad name when you make sweeping, derogatory comments about men." Focus on the behavior, not the person. Calling someone a racist or a bigot won't get anywhere—it will just erect more barriers. Sometimes just clarifying the comment will help the other person realize the error: "Am I clear in understanding that you believe all Irish people to be drunks?"

* Be open to criticism. If you have offended someone, don't get defensive. Listen to the person carefully and make sure you understand him or her. "So, it was offensive when I said that all Asians are bad drivers? Obviously, it's something I need to work on, and I'm sorry. Thanks for pointing it out."

* Keep relationships intact. "Joe said all blondes were dumb. What a jerk. I hope he enjoys *this* blonde not answering his phone," says one female coworker. Instead of Joe making the situation worse with another derogatory comment, he should simply apologize and then say something like, "I know this is awkward, but I'd like to keep working with you."

* Draw the line. If offensive remarks don't stop, at least make it clear you don't want them said around you. "I don't want

to hear racist or sexist jokes anymore. I hope you'll respect my wishes and not tell them in my presence." If you can, get a coworker who feels the same to support you.

* Be patient. Change won't happen overnight, but if you make a conscious effort to be more tolerant and to eliminate offensive workplace behavior, then others may learn from you. Keep speaking up when others are intolerant.

To further educate yourself, check out www.tolerance.org for more information.

23. Disrespecting a Mentor

You would probably feel very fortunate indeed if one day you were told you were getting a mentor. The thought of some gray-haired, kindly person with decades of knowledge saving you from the land mines and quicksand in the workplace would be a welcome event, wouldn't it?

But the days of the mature worker "bringing along" the young, talented worker are pretty much over. Organizations have flattened out their hierarchies, which makes it tougher for that kind of formal mentoring to take place. Executives often job-hop as often as younger workers, making it more difficult to find that silver-haired, senior employee willing to take you under his or her wing for an extended period of time.

Despite this development, mentoring relationships still exist and are considered quite valuable to a career. The difference is that mentoring relationships today are more fluid—they may be formed through connections in professional groups or other organizations and may last for a defined period of time.

Your boss probably has a mentor, and may have in fact had several different ones over the course of a career. Those in management understand that they rise through the ranks not only based on their job performance, but because of who they know and who is willing to put in a good word for them.

That's why the boss believes that mentors are so valuable to anyone aspiring to improve job performance, and that includes you. Without a mentor your career can stagnate because you stumble again and again through the shades of gray that exist in every workplace.

Bosses often do not have the time to steer every employee through the maze of office politics and career development. They know how important mentoring is; they expect employees to understand it too. Your boss wants you to grow from your mentoring experience just as you would any kind of training. Wasting the opportunity a mentor offers will only frustrate the boss because she sees you throwing away a golden opportunity for success. And remember: Your success is her success. When you don't make the most of a mentoring opportunity, you're impacting her career as well.

It's important to treat a mentor with respect. A mentor was not put on this earth to put up with whatever crap you dish out. Ignoring advice, being late for meetings with a mentor or refusing to one day become a mentor yourself are all signs of disrespect for the mentor and the process.

And if the boss catches wind of your behavior, watch out. She will not be happy that your unprofessional and ungrateful behavior could reflect poorly on her. Bosses understand how important maintaining good professional standing is both inside and outside your company, and disrespecting a mentor can damage not only your reputation, but possibly hers as well.

There are some basic rules of the mentoring relationship that if followed can lead to a beneficial outcome for both the mentor and you:

⋆ Choose the right mentor. Maybe you have the needed skills for the job, but your interactions with others could use some work. Since a mentor doesn't always have to be from your company or a member of your profession, consider a mentoring relationship with someone such as a spiritual leader or respected member of your community. Or, maybe you can't seem to grasp the next rung of the career ladder. A mentor with more workplace experience can help point out what you're doing right and what you're doing wrong. Professional organizations, trade associations or even alumni groups can help you find a mentor who can provide insights over the life of your career.

⋆ Find a mutual benefit. I don't consider myself a slouch at technology, but I know I have limitations. I learned a long time ago that I could coach younger workers on how to ask for a raise or get a promotion, while they helped me understand the latest high-tech advances.

My point is that when you find someone you think would make a good mentor, look for ways to offer something in return. Maybe you can give the mentor some insight into how things are "in the trenches," while the mentor offers you the "big picture" on company strategies.

⋆ Set goals. Let your mentor know what you hope to gain from the relationship. "I've been having trouble getting others to listen to me. I'm hoping you can help me understand how I can handle situations better so that my ideas will be heard and appreciated," you might say. Mentors like not only knowing what is expected of them but how long it might take. Remember that many mentors have busy lives and careers and may be more willing to be a mentor if they see an end in sight: "I thought we'd try this for nine months, then talk again about whether we think it needs to continue, or if I've learned enough to try things on my own," you can say.

* Pay it forward. Mentors have a sense of service to others or they wouldn't be helping you out. It's important to them to know they've had an impact and that their service will be passed on. Let them know that one day you hope to help someone else, if you haven't done so already.

24. Not Getting to Know Others in the Company

At work, it's often tempting to ignore the bigger picture. We drag ourselves into work and focus on getting through the tasks of the day. But if you don't widen your circle, then you run a real risk of becoming less useful. If you don't have a true understanding of what is going on not only within your immediate area but the company as a whole, then you have limited yourself and your potential to make a meaningful impact.

And that isn't something the boss likes to see happen. As I've mentioned before, no company and no individual can exist in a vacuum in today's fast-paced global marketplace. If you fail to connect with others in your company, then you fail to deliver the kind of performance that your boss expects.

I understand that it can be tough to walk outside your immediate comfort zone. Companies often are like high school cliques—departments stick together and tend to view "outsiders" with a certain level of distrust. Still, there are ways to make the foray into another area smoother and it begins with understanding a little something about yourself.

Dale Carnegie, the godfather of self-improvement, wrote *How to Win Friends and Influence People* in 1936. Since thirty million copies have sold to date, it's pretty obvious to me that a lot of people believe they need pointers on how to grow their personal appeal. And while dozens and dozens of similar books have been written since Carnegie's, they all state a basic principal: You have to put some effort into getting to know other people.

Emilio J. Castilla, a management professor at a top university, says managers care about you becoming familiar to others in the company because "if you're too embedded, then you don't have external benefits." In other words, the more people you know, the more valuable you are to your boss.

"Even if you know someone slightly, you still might be able to help them somehow in the future. This other employee you only met once might say, 'What was the name of that guy I met at that office party? I think he might be someone who could help me out . . .'" Castilla says.

Some of you may be groaning at this point at the thought of having to meet new people. Well, suck it up. You can be grumpy and inaccessible and a loner on your own time. When you're at work you have responsibilities, and one of those is to do your job to the best of your ability. If you're hiding in a cubicle or venturing outside your workstation only to visit the restroom or hit the Starbucks downstairs, you have to make some changes.

Remember that being "well connected" within the company will not only help your career but increase your value to the boss. If she knows that you have the inside skinny on what's going on company-wide, she will see you as part of the bigger picture in her own success.

Networking within your company is not much different than when you network with those in other companies. Some good rules of thumb to make contact:

★ Focus on the other person. Andrea Nierenberg, a management consultant and networking expert, says that you must remember "everyone you meet is important."

  "Networking is about creating connections that could last a lifetime," she says. "Opportunities often come about from the least-expected sources. People make a mistake when they believe networking is about what *they* can get."

★ Plan ahead. If you're hesitant about meeting someone for the first time, ask someone—such as a human resources or public relations person—to introduce you. If you approach a person on your own, think of a good opening line about what you do, because that will interest the other person.

★ Pay attention. Try to get an impression of the other person so that you can commit his or her name and job to memory. Say the person's name the first time you meet. "It's nice to meet you, Ann." Ask open-ended questions, such as "How did you come to work in this department, Ann?" When it comes time to move on, make a polite exit. "It was nice speaking with you and learning about your job, Ann."

★ Understand challenges. Pay attention to the problems cited by your new contact in the department—not enough people to answer phones or to put away files or supplies? Too much paperwork overwhelming workers? Other workers will be much more willing to open up to someone who shows a sincere interest in the job and the challenges.

* Foster communication. Before leaving, ask the person what is the best way to reach him or her—e-mail, cell phone, voice message or in person? This way if you come across interesting industry news, or other information that might affect the person, you can send it along and continue the connection.

* Offer something. "Is there anything I—or my department—can do to help you with your job?"

* Follow up. After meeting someone, jot down some notes that will help you remember the person, and anything he or she mentioned that might be of help in the future. Make sure you file contact information so that you can easily reach the person in the future, even if it's just to say "hello" and get an update on the department's projects.

25. Giving Feedback That Is Deliberately Hurtful

Dear Anita,
At work, I told a woman that she was so slow that a snail
could beat her in a footrace. People seemed surprised I said
it but I don't care. I told it like it was and I don't think I
have anything to apologize for. If more people were honest,
we wouldn't have all these problems in the world. How can I
get more people at work to see that honesty is still the best
policy?
Straight Talker

Dear Talker,
I agree there's not enough honesty in the world. But
I also think there's such a thing as being so honest it's
like being hit upside the head with a blunt instrument. Your
intention, I'm afraid, was not to be honest but to pee on
someone's parade. Your observation did nothing but demean
another person. Since you seem to be big on old adages,

how about this one: If you can't say anything nice, don't say anything at all.

Anita

In a survey of 775 people who were the targets of incivility at work—looking at everything from rudeness and insensitivity to disrespect—more than half said they had lost work time worrying about an ugly incident with a coworker, or the future possibility of one. While there were no incidents of physical aggression, the survey found that problems cited by workers included sending a nasty or demeaning note, making accusations about a lack of knowledge, undermining credibility in front of others and being shouted at.[11]

The survey also found that nearly half thought about quitting to avoid the incivility, while some 12 percent actually changed jobs.

"The exit data on why people quit jobs is not because they don't like their boss, but because they couldn't get along with coworkers," says Arthur H. Bell, a professor of management communications. "One of the biggest bottom-line costs is when a person is driven out by language."

That means that if the boss hears you make a snide comment to someone in a meeting, if the boss hears you berating a coworker or if the boss catches wind of complaints about your rude attitude toward others, then you're going to be considered a problem. The boss will be afraid to let you venture into polite company, which means you won't be allowed to work with important clients or work on key projects dependent on teamwork and cooperation.

Further, he certainly won't let you within spitting distance of

---

[11] Christine Pearson, University of North Carolina-Chapel Hill, Kenan-Flagler Business School

anyone important in the company. And why should he? Your behavior is not only immature and unprofessional, but indicates that you have little control over an ugly temperament. Bosses are judged by their department's performance, and teams who do not work well together have lower productivity, higher turnover and lower quality work. The boss cannot afford to have anyone impacting the work in a negative way through hurtful words and actions because then he'll have some explaining to do to his boss.

"The boss runs the ship, and the boss can be evaluated by what goes on in the ship," Bell explains.

Maybe, however, you think that "telling it like it is" is something to be admired in the workplace. Maybe you believe that you are just being honest and your feedback should be valued by others, not scorned. And probably you also believe that if someone can't take the heat, then he or she should get out of the kitchen. The workplace is no place for weenies, right?

But did you ever stop to think that you're the problem? Because if you were really thinking like an adult, then you'd stop the kind of behavior exhibited in schoolyards every day. It's easier, after all, to keep others from threatening you in some way by keeping them beaten down with ugly words and actions. So, instead of relying on your intelligence and your skills, you rely on being negative to others, by attacking their confidence and their ability to do the job. Is that the action of a gutsy person or a weak one?

Marshall Goldsmith, an executive coach to top CEOs, points out that "claiming you're just being honest is an excuse."

"There's a difference between honesty and destructive disclosure," Goldsmith says. "You can think what you want but that doesn't mean you need to tell someone. Always ask yourself: 'Is this going to help the company, the customer, the person you're talking to or the person you're talking about?' If the answer is no, no, no, no, then don't say it. Even if it's true, so what? It doesn't help anything."

So, if you want to turn your feedback into something that impresses others, you need to do the following:

★ Avoid personal attacks. Perhaps the person getting feedback from you is not a favorite of yours. But despite what you feel, focus on the work. Don't waste everyone's time by letting old grudges or biases get in the way. Instead of saying, "It's just like you to spend more time drinking coffee and flirting than getting the work done," you say, "The deadline on this was missed so let's find a way to make it up to the customer."

★ Look for the impact. If an issue doesn't impact your job then it's probably a good idea to keep your nose out of it. If you do somehow get involved, try to ask questions so that you get a better insight about what is happening and why.

★ Know what you're talking about. Always make sure you have your facts straight and don't rely on third-party information when offering feedback. If you don't offer feedback that is valid, then your opinions could be dismissed in the future.

★ Judge not. When you're asked for feedback, don't use words or phrases that judge or evaluate. Instead of saying, "If you weren't so unorganized, you would have caught the budget mistake sooner," say, "Accounting says we've gone over budget so we need to come up with a way to cut costs."

Avoid making your feedback some kind of power struggle—it shouldn't threaten someone's self-esteem or job security.

★ Be specific. Avoid "kitchen sink" discussions where all kinds of issues are brought up. "This report is full of errors because you always get in such a hurry. You're always late to work, and then you have to rush through the monthly reports and you aren't willing to stay late because you want to run around with your friends . . ." Instead, say something like: "I see that last week's report had at least three factual errors. Let's build some extra time into the schedule so that there's time to proofread the work before turning it in." Avoid such words as "always" and "should" and try to keep the accusatory "you" out of your tone.

★ Pick the right time. When the stress level is high and deadlines are looming, don't try to offer feedback to anyone. Wait until things are calmer and messages can be received in a positive atmosphere.

★ Be realistic. Don't offer feedback on something the person can't control or change, such as physical appearance or limitations.

★ Bury the past. Hindsight is always 20/20—offering feedback on something that happened in the past isn't productive. Focus on what steps can be taken today to fix a problem.

26. Fostering an Offensive Workspace

It bugs your boss when your workstation is offensive, just like it bugs her when you dress inappropriately. It's not something she can avoid. If she wants to stop and speak with you, she wants to do it without being assaulted by the smell of the leftover hamburger (with extra onions) you had for lunch, which is now fermenting in your trash can. She wants to have a work-related conversation without being eyeball to eyeball with your signed poster of the Hooters girls. She wants to be able to introduce you to clients or others in the company without having them wonder about your "SpongeBob SquarePants for President" sign posted over your computer.

Your boss doesn't care if you have a framed picture of your family, a nice dieffenbachia and a cup of coffee at your workstation. She wants you to be comfortable while you work, but at the same time, you must remember that your workstation is company property. Your chair, your desk, your bulletin board, your computer, your phone and your file cabinet are not your personal property. Doing your best to re-create your rec room at home shows a lack of professional responsibility and awareness of your role within the organization.

Remember that as you can be judged by the company you keep, you also can be judged by the cubicle you keep. Here are some dos and don'ts of keeping your workstation on the right track:

⋆ Do keep it clean. I've already discussed keeping your workstation organized (see #15), but it's also a smart idea to give it a good cleaning every now and then. If you can write your name in the grime, you know that it's time to get out the cleaning supplies. You have the added benefit of knowing that keeping your computer monitor free of dust will help cut down on eyestrain and wiping down your phone and keyboard with disinfecting wipes will help cut down on germs, especially those that spread colds and the flu.

⋆ Don't forget the smells. If you eat at your workstation, deposit your leftover food and wrappings in the lunchroom garbage. (And honestly, can't you eat that garlic chicken somewhere else?) Keep your area clear of smells that might be offensive to others, such as heavy colognes, hair products and candles.

⋆ Keep it down. Whether you're talking on the phone or speaking to someone, try to keep your voice down. Tight working spaces mean that even a short conversation can be distracting to others if you're not using a quiet tone.

⋆ Don't make personal statements. Save your political, social or religious items for your home. Employers are leery of discrimination claims and prefer to have such items (calendars, coffee cups, figurines, photos, etc.) left at home.

★ Do remember your image. A vacation photo of you in an abbreviated swimsuit leering drunkenly at the camera with your friends is not the kind of image you want at work. Cramming your workspace with too many personal mementos makes it appear you put more effort into your personal life than your work life.

★ Do watch the content. No cheerleader posters, swimsuit model screensavers, beer calendars or coffee cups declaring "Work Sucks."

★ Do be resourceful. Calling out "How do you spell . . . ?" or "Do you know the phone number . . . ?" is bothersome to those around you. Try to be resourceful in finding information so you don't have to bother coworkers with things you could find out on your own through a little effort.

★ Don't play loud music. If you choose to listen to music, use earphones. Still, make sure the music isn't so loud that others can hear it despite the headset or so loud you can't hear others speaking to you. It's rude to be so tuned in to the music that you don't answer questions or phones.

The key is to remember that work often is a stressful place. The more you do to minimize your contribution to that anxiety, and the more you demonstrate to the boss that you are respectful of others and your company, the better off you—and your career—will be.

27. Gossiping

*"Gossip is the art of saying nothing in a way
that leaves practically nothing unsaid."*
—Walter Winchell

We all know that every workplace has gossips. People get juiced up on gossip, sort of like gulping an extra double chocolate espresso with whipped cream. It gets the blood pumping and the heart racing. In the workplace, people gossip about who got a promotion and why, who got into an argument, who messed up, who is about to be fired, whose kid got arrested for breaking and entering and who was seen at a local pub, drunk as a skunk.

But the problem with workplace gossip (other than the fact it is often hurtful and untrue) is that bosses see it as a big waste of time. They don't like employees gossiping because it takes away from valuable work time. They don't like gossip because it forces them to spend valuable hours putting out "fires" caused by misinformation. Rumors and speculation all undermine the team concept in the workplace, fueling distrust and disloyalty among coworkers, which affects efficiency and productivity.

"The bottom line is that gossip destroys trust, encourages

people not to be truthful with one another and makes them judg-mental," says James W. Tamm, a former judge and expert on dis-pute resolution. "All those things weaken the workplace."

That's why if you gossip at work, you could become the focus of the boss's ire, not only because it is disruptive but because it can lead to problems—including legal ones.

Specifically, employers have been sued by workers claiming that gossip caused them psychological trauma on the job. Further, employees can claim they were sexually harassed or had their civil rights violated because of gossip, and some local laws make it ille-gal to harass people based on things like sexual orientation. Bosses know that legal entanglements are something companies want to avoid, so they will try to head off potential problems—and that could mean firing an employee who gossips.

At this point, some may argue that gossip is as necessary to the workplace at breathing. After all, it's important to know who is doing what, isn't it? Understanding all the players and what's going on in various areas is critical to career success, isn't it? Well, yes—and no. There's a difference between networking and gossip. Net-working is where you establish positive relationships with other people, fostering communication and understanding in order to improve your performance. Gossip is unnecessary, harmful and negative—it's just a chance to dish some dirt.

In order to protect your career and your employer from poten-tial legal problems, avoid being labeled a gossip. You need to do several things:

★ Stop being available. Don't get caught in the lunchroom or around the water cooler by someone who has a tale to spread.

"Oh, sorry . . . I've got to run. I'm on a deadline," you say, quickly moving away. At the same time, don't get cornered in your office or workspace by someone who wants to gossip. "Gee, I've got to get this done or I'm never going to get out of here tonight," you say, turning away. Begin working, even if you have to pretend to be busy.

★ Be honest. Before you say anything at work, make sure it's the truth. Don't fabricate or embellish facts in order to make an issue more interesting. Your speculation can lead to very unhappy repercussions if the boss traces the rumor or gossip to your doorstep.

★ Be frugal. You don't have to offer a comment or opinion on everything. If you don't have anything positive to contribute, don't say anything. Be careful with your words so that gossips know you aren't willing to chatter about just anything.

★ See it in print. As a journalist, I've been taught to check and recheck facts. There's nothing worse than seeing an error in print. It's there for all time and you just feel rotten about it. Before you speak or listen to someone else at work, think about how you would feel to have your words on the front page of the newspaper the next morning. If you'd be OK with it, go ahead. But if you'd be ashamed or embarrassed then you know to keep your thoughts to yourself.

★ The Golden Rule. How would you feel if someone gossiped about you at work? Look at your own values before you pass along half-truths or listen to them.

★ Meet it head on. Many gossips are very clever—they may not directly say what they mean, only offering hints. Try questioning them: "What do you mean exactly by that?" "Can you tell me where and when that happened and if you were present?" This kind of attitude should curb a gossip's tongue.

Finally, remember that if you can cut out your gossiping time— and head off those who want to spend time gossiping—you may just find yourself getting more done in less time. What boss wouldn't appreciate a worker who is more efficient and productive?

28. Not Giving—or Accepting— an Apology

As children, we're taught that saying "I'm sorry" goes a long way toward getting us out of trouble. Spill a cup of milk? "I'm sorry, Mommy," we say. As we get older, we learn to say "I'm sorry" to friends when we hurt their feelings. As adults, we say, "I'm sorry" for everything from failing to pick up the dry cleaning to expressing sympathy for the loss of a loved one.

Still, in the workplace the simple words "I'm sorry" become more complicated. Some workers believe that apologizing is tantamount to admitting they're idiots. Some believe apologizing puts them in a position of weakness and some would rather walk naked through rush-hour traffic than admit they owe a coworker an apology.

At the same time, even if an apology is given, some people seem to have a difficult time accepting it. I once had a colleague who refused to accept an apology from me after I inadvertently hurt his feelings. He simply looked at me, stone-faced. For six months, he refused to talk to me. He would ask others to relay messages to me or ignore me when I walked in a room. I have to say the experience left a really foul taste in my mouth, and when for some reason one day he decided to forgive me and accept my apology, I no longer cared.

I think it's important to understand how important giving—and accepting—the apology is in the workplace today. It's sort of like the marriage counselor who tells a couple never to go to bed mad at one another because letting problems fester without a timely resolution can lead to divorce. If you can't get past difficulties at work by learning how to offer and accept an apology, you could get stuck in a rut of resentment and hard feelings that makes it impossible to work effectively with someone. This inability to move on could lead the boss to conclude that you're not ready to move up, either.

Marshall Goldsmith, an executive coach to CEOs, says that people often have a difficult time giving or accepting an apology "because we have this incredible need to win—people are so driven to prove they're right that even though they know what they should do, they don't."

If you are ready to move on, however, and need to issue an apology or accept one, some key things you need to know:

★ Don't go overboard. Think Eddie Haskell. Nobody likes an overly effusive apology that drips with false sincerity. And don't make the apology about you by listing all the rotten things you've done in your life and how you got to this point. It only embarrasses others, and takes the punch out of your apology. "Tell the person that you know you can't change the past, but you can change the future," Goldsmith says.

★ Be specific. Make it clear that you understand how your action caused a problem. "I'm sorry I didn't deliver the mes-

sage in a timely manner, causing you to miss the meeting."
Don't make a bunch of excuses that just muddy the water
and dilute the message.

⋆ Offer a remedy. If you've goofed it's always best to offer a
solution so that others feel you've given the issue some consideration. You can say, "I'm sorry I failed to deliver your
message on time. From now on, I plan on sending you an
e-mail as soon as I take a message."

⋆ Don't fidget. You're not a five-year-old, so always look
someone in the eye when offering an apology. If appropriate, offer a handshake when you're done. An apology can be
issued via e-mail or telephone if necessary, but always try to
make an apology in person because it simply shows a lot of
class, maturity and professionalism to do so.

⋆ Keep it private. Don't apologize just so others can see what
a big person you are. The purpose of saying "I'm sorry" is
to erase hard feelings and reestablish communication with
another person. If the person feels he or she is being put on
display for your performance as a contrite soul, then you've
only compounded the problem. You can ask the person to
step into a quiet hallway or catch the person before or after
work when others aren't as likely to interrupt.

⋆ Understand it's not about you. When you apologize, you
should not somehow make the other person feel sorry for
you. "I'm sorry I didn't deliver the message, but my girl-
friend broke up with me and took my dog." By whining
about your own life, you take the focus off the apology and
the other person.

If you're in the position where someone is offering you an apology, you need to remember that mature, professional and gracious adults can say, "Thank you for your apology," or "Forget it! We all make mistakes," or even "OK." Sometimes, you may need to even tender an apology in return: "I understand. In fact, I'd like to apologize for not notifying you sooner we might have a problem with the delivery date."

Remember, even if you are still a little miffed (or seriously ticked off) about an incident, any attempt at an apology should be accepted—taking the high ground at work always pays off in the end.

Part Four

Clueless in Seattle . . . and Cleveland . . . and Topeka . . . Bosses Don't Give Leadership Roles to Those Who Lack Maturity and Common Sense

Your boss often gets quizzed by her boss about a variety of things, including staff development. Who looks like they could assume more responsibilities? Who isn't progressing? What is being done to assure that key employees are being developed for leadership roles?

When she's being questioned, your boss probably has visions of you and others swimming around in her head. She remembers the time you burst into tears during a disagreement with another worker and how you love to gossip. She has a clear memory of Jim's lousy presentation in front of a client and how he dresses like a slob. And, of course, how can she ever forget Tricia's drunken rendition of "Crazy" at the holiday party and her unintelligible progress reports?

Then she envisions Jack, who stumbled a bit, but is now a valuable part of the team. Elaine too, she thinks, is really on top of things and capable of standing up for herself and overcoming obstacles. Both of these employees, your boss tells her boss, have good leadership potential.

The top boss probably then issues a plan of action to your boss: Give Jack and Elaine more leadership roles.

Notice how you, Jim and Tricia didn't enter into the leadership equation? That's because your actions have led the boss to conclude that you need more supervision—not more responsibility.

"Unfair!" you may cry. "Why are our mistakes held against us, while Jack and Elaine are put on the leadership track?"

Why? Because the employees who overcome their mistakes and move on to become consistent, valuable performers are much less wear and tear on the boss. A boss does not want to handhold an employee through the leadership process and possibly face future embarrassment in front of others because of consistent failures.

It's sort of like when you take a significant other home to meet your family for the first time.

"Please don't embarrass me, please don't embarrass me," you beg silently to your loved ones. "Please don't tell stupid stories about me, be obnoxious, rude or pass gas. Please, please, *please*."

That's how the boss feels. She silently begs you not to embarrass her with your ineptness, your immaturity or your lack of preparation. (She would probably also appreciate you not passing gas.)

But if you do, you can bet she won't forget it. You might be able to diminish the memory if you quickly move to rectify it, but if you continue to have the same bad judgment, you will be engraved in her memory like a bad tattoo.

Do you have a plan of action when it becomes clear you're not being targeted for bigger and better things? Do you even know what can torpedo your leadership aspirations? If not, it's time to find out and develop a plan so that next time the boss makes a list for the leadership track, you're at the top.

29. Crying at Work

Dear Anita,
Recently a coworker told me to "shut up" and I burst into
tears. It really hurt my feelings (I'm quite sensitive). My boss
told me I needed to stop crying at work, and that just made
me cry harder. Is it really that bad to be so emotionally
available?
Full of Tears

Dear Tears,
There's nothing wrong with being emotionally available
with, say, your schnauzer or your grandma. But tears at work
make everyone uncomfortable. If you've got to cry, wait until
you get home and then feel free to bawl your head off over
the spilled milk.
Anita

It is true that if someone cries at work, it's more likely to be a
woman rather than a man. But it's also true that women who cry
aren't doing it because they're weak. They're usually doing it

because a really strong emotion—such as anger or outrage—has been triggered.

But that's where women make a big mistake. If a woman is mad or outraged, she should say so. Crying doesn't tell anyone anything except that she has lost control. Instead, she should put her feelings into words: "You know, it really makes me angry when you yell at me." Then she should state what she wants to happen next: "I expect to be addressed in a calm, civilized manner and I don't want to discuss this until you do."

Early in my career, I was in a situation at work where I cried in front of my boss and my boss's boss. Fortunately, they chalked it up to the fact that I was coming down with the flu. But when I shared what happened with my mom, she gave me some valuable advice: "Get out of there if you feel like you're going to cry."

Other women I've spoken with agree. If you feel the tears start, make your exit.

"I need to cool down and have some time to gather my thoughts. I'll get back to you," you can say, as your feet make tracks. In fact, such a strategy can actually bolster a woman's position since she leaves others believing that she is not willing to back down and feels strongly about her position.

Corinne L. Gediman, an adult learning specialist and corporate trainer, says that while people are becoming more understanding when a man or woman "wells up," crying at work still means "that a person's competency will be questioned."

"I think most people just think: 'Thank God that's not me,'" she says of an emotionally stressed worker.

If you've ever seen the movie *Broadcast News*, you may remember the character played by Holly Hunter, a tough television producer who seemed to always be confident and in control. But she often would find a quiet place and just bawl her head off. After a few minutes she would wipe her eyes, blow her nose and head back to work. I think most of us could identify with her in some way. Even if you're a man and not prone to tears, unleashing emotional stress can be quite cleansing. Sort of like an internal radiator flush.

That's why I'm not saying you should never cry. A good sob can often replenish your emotional reserves and stiffen your backbone. But if you've got to cry, then for heaven's sake, don't do it at work. If you've cried at work in the past, now is time to make a plan so it won't happen again.

Remember, crying makes some bosses miserable, many uncomfortable and others impatient—but they all wish you wouldn't do it. They know that other employees—both men and women—see it as a sign of weakness or a reason for pity. Either way, crying at work doesn't help you develop the kind of reputation you need to be seen as a leader. The boss understands that others must see you as strong, assured and capable in order to make decisions that will be supported and followed.

Here are some ways you can keep crying under control at work:

* Learn your triggers. Maybe it's a certain employee at work that really gets your goat, or perhaps it's when you feel unfairly targeted for criticism. Think about how you can handle such situations better. Write down some responses that don't attack anyone; they simply state your position. Practice these statements until you feel comfortable and confident saying them.

* Look for support. If you fear you may have trouble keeping tears at bay in a certain situation, try to get a colleague to

support you. Sometimes by just having someone near you in a meeting you can gain strength and get through a tough time. Or, the colleague can help deflect attention away from you if you do start to get emotional and need a moment to regain control.

★ Speak up. Tears are the by-product of powerful feelings. Why not channel that energy into some powerful action or words instead? You might say, "Calling me unorganized is not only untrue but it doesn't solve this problem. I've worked very hard on this project and I'm not going to let it be derailed at this point. Please excuse me while I get to work on some ideas."

★ Take care of yourself. One of the reasons I cried at work was indeed because I was coming down with the flu. But I should have realized I wasn't feeling well and it wasn't the time to have a talk with my bosses about my job duties. Don't get yourself into tough situations at work when you're tired, hungry, ill or under a lot of stress. If someone wants to talk to you about something you fear will trigger tears, use some excuse to be by yourself at least ten minutes to do some deep breathing, take a walk or get a nutritious snack to boost your energy reserves.

★ Plan your recovery. If you do cry before you can make an escape, head for a quiet place to collect yourself such as outdoors, a quiet conference room or even the janitor's closet. Once you calm down, try to do something to make you feel better such as brushing your teeth, washing your face or combing your hair. If people ask you if something is wrong after seeing your face, say your allergies are acting up. Don't get into a discussion with anyone else when your emotions are raw, and definitely don't put anything in writing when you're upset. If you want to call a friend or family member, do it where you won't be overheard. And finally, if you just can't get control of yourself, take some sick time and go home for the day.

30. Caving In to a Bully

Everyone has a story of being the target of a bully as a kid. Maybe some older boy stole your lunch money every day, or a girl made fun of the way you dressed. But often this bullying came to an end as you grew up and went to another school, or a parent or teacher put a stop to the bullying behavior.

But in the workplace, it's not that simple. While it would certainly be nice to complain to our mom, who would then call the boss, who would then put a stop to the bully's behavior, it doesn't happen that way in the working world. In the working world, the boss expects you to handle a bully on your own. And here's why: Because if you become the target of a bully once, then it's likely to happen again. The boss believes that if he has to rescue you once, he'll have to do it again.

Further, the boss knows that those who are given leadership roles must be able to stand up for themselves. If you cave in to a bully, it's a signal to the boss that there may be underlying confidence problems and an unwillingness to handle confrontation and conflict—something that any leader must deal with effectively.

Who are workplace bullies? According to research,[12] both men and women can be bullies, and it can take place in any kind of workplace, from a manufacturing plant to a high-tech firm. In their private lives, bullies can be church deacons or soccer moms, but at work, they are aggressive.

"Bullying is a silent epidemic that affects one in six workers," says Gary Namie, a workplace-bullying expert. "It is witnessed by nearly 80 percent of workers who don't do anything about it. It's a dirty little secret."

Who is most likely to become the target of a bully? Namie says targets often have a strong sense of equity, justice and integrity and a very strong belief in what they believe to be right and wrong. Bullies are the opposite—they feel inadequate even though they strut around like peacocks. They are secretly intimidated by the target's intelligence, creativity and confidence. In order to deal with what they perceive to be a threat, bullies begin spreading rumors and innuendo about the target and may try to sabotage work.

As Namie says, bullies often target the most talented in the workplace because "the dolts don't threaten anybody."

That's why if you're talented and creative and have been bullied once, chances are good it could happen again.

"The targets of bullies often are people who are strong and independent and talented and believe they can tough it out," Namie says. "But once the bullying starts, most can only stay 16.5 months because it costs them their health."

What are some behaviors that may prompt a bully to make you

[12] The U.S. Hostile Workplace Survey 2000, Campaign Against Workplace Bullying

a target? Research shows that making statements where you put yourself down such as, "I'm bad with computers—I'm so dumb," or "You guys should just go on without me because I'm no help and I'll just slow you down," put a bully on alert. At the same time, behaviors that may betray a lack of confidence such as talking too slow (which allows a bully to interrupt) or too fast (betraying nervousness) also attract a bully's notice.

The nonverbal cues also play a role: Bullies look for those who don't walk confidently with head held high, or those who fail to use gestures to emphasize a point, as if they're afraid to call attention to themselves. Bullies also will test you by invading your personal space and seeing whether you put them back in their place.

Namie adds that bullies also are lazy and look for easy marks. That's why they often will try their intimidation on new employees because they know the vulnerabilities that go along with being the new kid on the block. Still, research shows that some 75 percent of the workforce does not tolerate being controlled by another person, and a bully will back off when resistance is shown—even if it's from a new employee.

If you become the target of a bully, Namie says you should do the following:

* Stop listening to the bully's lies and verbal assaults. You did nothing wrong and don't need to feel ashamed.

* Break through your fears. Even if you do it for only one week, it's better to confront your worst fear and stand up to the bully. Procrastination only makes the problem worse.

★ Assert your right to be treated with respect regardless of who you are and where you rank.

★ Demand respect directly from the bully whenever you interact. You owe it to yourself.

★ Document the bully's misconduct. Report him/her to anyone who will listen. Break the silence.

★ Rally witnesses and coworkers to help defend you, to shame the cowardly bully-tyrant.

Bullying—whether it happens when we're kids or when we're adults—can be very difficult. If you need help coping, don't hesitate to ask for professional help. Your company's employee assistance program (EAP) can offer resources, as well as community mental health organizations. Also, check out www.bullybusters .org for more strategies and information.

31. Failing to Learn from Mistakes

Sometimes you can keep your little boo-boos quiet. Maybe only one or two people find out that you screwed up. Perhaps the mistake is so widely known you're surprised it's not on CNN. But I understand that it's often embarrassing to make a mistake, and sometimes humiliating, and sometimes it just royally pisses you off.

Still, despite what you may be feeling, it's important that you handle a mistake correctly. Your boss is looking beyond the error—she's taking into account how you react to it, how you recover from it and how you learn from it. She doesn't want to see you yelling, or sobbing, or whining, or cursing, or blaming someone else. She sure as heck doesn't want to see you ignore it. What she wants to see is a willingness to not only correct it (if possible), but the development of a strategy to learn from it and make sure it doesn't happen again. You must understand that your inability to handle a mistake may lead the boss to conclude that you are not self-directed enough to lead others.

Here are some key things to remember about mistakes:

★ Accept responsibility. Nothing will be gained from trying to blame someone else for your mistake. Such a strategy will certainly prompt hostility from the person blamed and it will foster disrespect and distrust from others. Plus, the mistake only will be compounded in the boss's eyes when your lie is brought to light. It's the kind of thing that can get you fired.

★ Respond accordingly. You may be under close scrutiny when it's learned you goofed. Others will be interested to see how you react—any hyperventilating, fainting or foaming at the mouth? Imagine the respect you will garner when you react professionally and competently.

★ Investigate. Try to get to the bottom of what happened and why. Avoid making any assumptions, since those may stop you from learning the real truth. Only by uncovering all the facts can you put an effective strategy in place to prevent you from making the same mistake twice.

★ Consider changes. Maybe a practice you've been using really isn't bulletproof and either needs to be altered or scrapped altogether. Leaders often must respond and react in a timely manner to different situations—the boss will be watching to see if you're stuck in a rut and making the same goofs over and over or if you're making changes as needed.

★ Laugh when you can. There may be something funny about your error that you can use to lighten the situation.

★ Be flexible. Once you decide how you can avoid making the same mistake again, don't be so sold on the idea that you become inflexible. Your boss wants you to think on your feet—it shows her you are willing to constantly adjust and learn in order to avoid errors.

32. Being Unable to Overcome Obstacles

No job is a cakewalk. Everyone seems to have something to whine about, including earning too much money. (I'm not making this up.)

One survey[13] in fact, found that executives had heard some real dillies about why employees left a job:

*   "An employee left because he didn't like the smell of the office."

*   "One guy said he was making too much money and didn't feel like he was worth it." (See, I told you I wasn't making it up.)

*   "Someone left to join the circus."

*   "He just walked out without a peep. Until this day we have no idea why he left, nor were we able to contact him."

[13] Survey of 125 advertising executives and 125 senior marketing executives by the Creative Group, www.creativegroup.com

★ "One employee quit because he said he was overemployed."

★ "We had a guy who said he couldn't get up in the morning."

★ "An employee moved to Italy because she didn't like the outcome of the election."

★ "A worker didn't like to use the computer and said the job wasn't as glamorous as she thought."

Is it any wonder bosses get exasperated with workers who cannot seem to get past their navel-gazing long enough to get the work done? Workers who give up and take off the first time the job doesn't go exactly as they want?

As I mentioned in the beginning of this book, a boss does not hire you to fire you. He has a contract with you—an employment contract. As part of that contract, you do the work to the best of your ability and, in return, you get a paycheck.

But what many employees don't seem to understand is that no job is without its challenges or obstacles, and bosses believe you should know that. They have plenty of balls they're trying to juggle without hearing you whine about how you don't like to use computers, the office smells funny or you'd rather be fishing.

Stopping in your tracks every time something on the job goes contrary to what you want does not make the boss think of you as leadership material. Honestly, it probably makes him think of you as "needs-a-keeper" material. Organizations are more streamlined than ever before—they are as strong as the weakest link. And if you're dragging your feet because you can't get past an obstacle, then chances are you're going to be perceived as a weak link—if not the weakest link.

That's why it's so important to overcome obstacles. Not only will it make you a stronger and more capable member of the team, but coworkers will view you as leadership material—an important qualification if you want to get ahead. Further, your ability to get past obstacles will be a critical indicator to the boss that you're able to meet the expectations and goals of the employer without being easily derailed. He won't put you in a leadership position if he believes you can't find a way around, through or over roadblocks.

"For many decades, employers sought employees who were caretakers. That meant they wanted employees who went along, who were told what to do," says Al Siebert, the director of a training company that teaches flexibility. "Now, with so much change in the workplace, employers are looking for those who can reorient themselves quickly—people who adapt to change."

So let's consider what you need to do to develop skills that will help you overcome obstacles:

* Outline the worst-case scenario. By writing down the potential pitfalls or at least verbalizing them, you face your fears. Fear often immobilizes you, so once you face it you can be better equipped to overcome it.

* Be willing to fight. Don't just accept what happens. Ask yourself what other roads you can take. Did you know that it's estimated most sales are made after the fifth rejection? Keep thinking of ways to rephrase your questions, come up with new information or bring in other resources. Don't give up the first time the going gets hard.

* Envision success. Keep your eye on the prize, whether it's nabbing a big contract or winning over a difficult customer.

When an obstacle pops up, make sure you have a clear idea of what the payoff will be once you get past it.

★ Bounce back. Your boss doesn't want to see you defeated by an obstacle—he wants to see you more determined than ever to succeed. Keep a sense of humor about it and the boss will see it as a positive sign that you might be temporarily down—but not out—of the game.

★ Be realistic. It's self-defeating to keep battering at an obstacle without knowing when to back off and rethink what you're doing. Maybe you really *do* need more training before trying for that promotion.

★ Get input. You don't always have to take the advice of someone else, but it often helps you clarify your problem if you can get ideas from other people. This doesn't always have to be someone you work with. A lot of successful people rely on friends or family to get another perspective.

★ Invest in confidence. Read inspirational books about how others facing adversity overcame it, or attend events that foster well-being and confidence. Spend time with others who have succeeded and ask them to share their stories of how they dealt with problems.

33. Having Too Much— or Too Little—Confidence

Dear Anita,

My boss just gave a terrific project to some idiotic candy ass that hasn't been with this company half as long as I have. This person is such a suck-up it makes me want to puke—always smiling and bringing in doughnuts for everyone. If it weren't for me, this company would go down the toilet in six months. I'm thinking of just quitting—I could take all the big customers with me and I'm sure the people I work with would come to work for me. I'm practically running the place as it is. This way I'd at least get most of the profits. How much notice do you think I should give the boss?
Jammin' Jeff

Dear Jeff,
Your arrogant attitude about your own worth to the company obviously has worked against you. Hence, the candy ass grabs the brass ring while you hold on to some misguided notion that you run the joint single-handedly.

But all is not lost. It's time to realize that your preening overconfidence is not only obnoxious, but downright danger-ous to your career. The first thing you should do? Stop by the nearest Krispy Kreme and load up. (I'll take mine with choco-late.)

Anita

There's such a thing as being confident, and then there's such a thing as being *over*confident. If you're wondering about the difference, consider the thirteen-foot Burmese python that tried to eat a six-foot alligator in the Florida Everglades.

The python exploded.

Now *that's* overconfidence.

In the workplace, bosses like workers to have a "can do" atti-tude. If a worker is too confident, however, bosses get nervous. That's because they know overconfidence often breeds big prob-lems. Employees who expect too much for too little effort often be-lieve "it will get done" without any real plan of how it actually *is* going to get done.

Your overconfidence also will be seen as false bravado. Your boss is probably savvy enough to understand that if you're brag-ging and expressing too much confidence, then you could possibly be secretly insecure—or just a jerk. Either way, she will take note of the fact that coworkers may not like your attitude. (A couple of them may be plotting to take you down a notch or two, while others may just be patiently waiting for you to self-destruct.) Further, your boss is wise enough to understand that most of your peers will be unwilling to help you out of a dilemma, feeling it is just desserts for someone who spends more time boasting than getting the work done.

Psychologists say that someone who is overconfident is just so darn certain that things are going to go his or her way—even though there's a good chance they won't—that the person loses sight of reality and begins making promises that cannot be kept. Is it any wonder, then, that bosses don't feel they can trust the workers who cannot keep their feet grounded in reality, providing them with realistic predictions and outcomes?

"People who are overconfident usually want to control everything, but you can bet they will make huge mistakes," says James W. Tamm, a former judge and dispute resolution expert. "People don't want to work with them, and they don't trust them."

Still, it's just as aggravating to a boss to be faced with an employee with little confidence. The boss must often spend extra energy just getting a person to believe he or she can do the work before anything is actually accomplished. While some bosses may be willing to do this a time or two, no boss has the time to continually bolster a person's self-esteem.

"Those who are really unconfident don't really do anything but waste any talent they have," Tamm says. "They just sort of sit there like a bump on a log."

Remember that if a boss hired you in the first place, then she trusted you to get the job done. Demonstrating little confidence in yourself is sort of like saying, "Well, you obviously don't know what the heck you're doing if you hired me!" How do you think she will react to that? She may take it as a direct slap to her managerial abilities, and a clear indicator that you're not only unprepared to move up, but may be a prime candidate to move out.

The key here is striking the right balance in the confidence game. Being a bragging blowhard who has unrealistic expectations of success is just as bad as the simpering ninny who is afraid to stand on his or her own two feet.

"Being overconfident or lacking any confidence both are behaviors that are driven by the same basic underlying fear," Tamm says. "They both show a fear about self-worth."

If you are spending too much time boasting instead of getting the job done, or are frozen with your lack of confidence, here are ways to let the boss know that you're ready to step up and get the job done:

★ Get to work. If you're overconfident, you spend a lot of time just talking about what you're going to get done instead of really doing it. If you lack confidence, you may spend too much time worrying or whining about what you need to do instead of getting it done. When given an assignment, work up a plan of action with a timetable. List the people and resources you can turn to if you run into problems you cannot handle in a timely manner.

★ Welcome challenges. Set clear, attainable goals for yourself. And once you accomplish a task, look for the next goal. Focus on how problems can be overcome and how each time you learn from that process.

★ Talk the talk. Don't use overconfident phrases such as "I'm the best," or "No one can beat me," or become so cocky that you tell others, "I know more about it than you do, so you better do what I say," or "You better do it my way." At the same time, avoid self-defeating statements such as, "I'm not smart enough," or "This may not be right, but . . ." The key is to focus your energy on getting the job done: "I'm excited to take on the challenge of this project," or "I'm sure I can find a solution."

★ Understand that mistakes happen. Look at mistakes as a temporary detour. Don't blame someone else or pretend it didn't happen. Find a new way to achieve your goals instead of running and hiding. If you can't realistically look at why a mistake happened, you're probably destined to repeat it.

★ Get a fresh perspective. While the overconfident person may see a glass as not just half full, but overflowing, the unconfident person will see it as half empty (and probably cracked). It's important to develop a support system to see you through the tough times, but equally as useful to find something within yourself to help you bounce back. Maybe it's a spiritual exercise, walking your dog or working in your garden. But doing something you enjoy often can help you regain your equilibrium and bolster your confidence.

★ Be persistent. Perhaps you don't have great success each time you try something, but the fact that you continue to try tells the boss something about your character and your confidence.

As Calvin Coolidge said, "Nothing in the world can take the place of persistence. Talent will not; nothing is more common than unsuccessful men with talent. Genius will not; unrewarded genius is almost a proverb. Education will not; the world is full of educated derelicts. Persistence and determination alone are omnipotent. The slogan 'press on' has solved and always will solve the problems of the human race."

Finally, look at levelheaded confidence as something to enjoy. While having too much confidence isn't worthwhile because you create unrealistic expectations that lead to disappointment for you and others, neither is it good to be a wilting lily that lets life pass by with barely a whimper. Hit the confidence mark that is honest and true for you.

In the words of another great American philosopher, Joe Namath: "When you have confidence, you can have a lot of fun. And when you have fun, you do amazing things."

34. Neglecting to Write Things Down

When I was in college, I was given the assignment by my school newspaper to cover a political fund-raising dinner with Richard Nixon scheduled as the guest speaker. This was an amazing opportunity—I was one of the hundreds of young journalists who went into the business after watching Watergate unfold. To get to see and hear the president who resigned after journalists exposed wrongdoings in his administration was something I would not have missed for anything in the world.

Armed with my reporter's notebook and a tape recorder, I sat in a roped-off area to the side of the stage where Nixon spoke. (As you can imagine, Nixon wasn't too keen on having journalists anywhere near him and we were told in no uncertain terms by the Secret Service to stay behind the rope.)

Nixon, reading from a prepared paper, was speaking too fast to take detailed notes by hand. I was grateful I had thought to bring the tape recorder, which I had switched on the minute he began to speak.

The next day sitting in my college newspaper office, I turned on the tape recorder to begin transcribing Nixon's speech so I could write my story.

"L . . . aaaaa . . ." I heard.

I stopped the tape and then hit "play" again.

"Grrrr . . ."

After a couple more attempts, I broke out in a cold sweat. The president who was at the center of an event that launched me into journalism was speaking as if he had a mouthful of marbles. I realized that the tape recorder's batteries had been dying during Nixon's speech. I had nothing useable on tape.

I quickly scrambled through my written notes. Very sketchy. Nothing too complete. I had attended my first presidential speech as a working journalist, and I had blown it.

I was sick.

Once I calmed down enough to think clearly, I realized that other journalists had been present. I quickly made some calls and found my reporting brethren to be sympathetic to my plight. A couple of them shared their notes so that I could fill in the holes from my own written ones, and I was able to put together a story.

To this day, even if I use a tape recorder, I still take complete notes by hand. Some sources have looked at me kind of strangely, wondering why I'm bothering to write it all down when I have a tape recorder running, but I'll never forget Nixon's slurred voice on that tape.

It certainly would have been convenient if I could have just given Nixon a call after I discovered my error. "Listen, Dick," I'd say. "Got a little problem here with the tape recorder so I was just wondering if you could repeat your speech for me. You know how it is when you tape-record conversations . . ."

Yeah, right. I'm sure Nixon would have appreciated that just as much as when you show up at your boss's side to say, "You know that thing you told me? Well, I can't quite remember what you said and I was wondering if you could go over it one more time . . ."

Bosses don't like going over it one more time. They don't like repeating things to workers who fail to write it down the first time. It's a waste of their time. You interrupt what they're doing to make them backtrack in their thoughts, possibly forcing them to search for their own notes on the subject. And God forbid, if you don't write it down the second time they tell you, you can bet your bottom dollar they're going to blow a gasket if you come to them a third time.

Relying on your own memory and recall ability is a tricky thing. It always amazes me when I go to a restaurant with friends or family. The friendly waiter approaches, and begins taking orders. Someone wants extra lemon in the tea. Another person wants no cheese, but extra mustard on a sandwich. Still another person wants the salad dressing on the side with no croutons or onions on the salad. The entire time the waiter is smiling—and not writing down a single word.

"Shouldn't you be writing this down?" I sometimes ask. "Can you really remember all that?"

The waiter, usually much younger than me, smiles. "Oh, I never forget," the waiter says.

And sometimes that is true. But more often than not, the extra lemon never arrives for the tea, there is no mustard or cheese on the sandwich, but plenty of croutons and onions on the salad. Alas, the salad dressing does arrive—but it is the wrong kind.

It's irritating, but usually we just sort of make do. We don't want to send the orders back, too hungry and often too rushed to wait to see what might arrive on the next attempt. But we don't tip as much as we might have, taking the opportunity to send a silent little message to the waiter that next time he needs to *write it down.*

Bosses often feel the same way. Maybe you don't write down his instructions but you still manage to get it—sort of. But because he's pressed for time because his boss is pushing him to get something done, he just takes what you've done and tries to fix it. You can bet, however, that when it comes time for your "tip"—such as a raise or a promotion—your lack of attention is going to be noted.

Failing to write down what the boss says when giving instructions also bugs a boss because he sees it as a sign of disrespect. Your avoidance of taking notes tells him that you don't think what he's saying is important, because if it was, you would write it down.

I'm not saying you should write down every word the boss says. Not only is that impractical, but the boss may become annoyed as he is forced to talk to the top of your head, which is bent over a notepad while you scribble industriously. What I am saying is that taking notes in the right way and at the right time can not only make the boss appreciate your efforts, it can save you both time and energy because you have a clear idea of what you're supposed to accomplish.

You should always take notes in the following situations:

* When issues are time sensitive. If a customer needs a quote by a certain time or a project is due on a specific date, write down the information.

* When the boss calls you into his office. Usually he has specific items on his mind, so grab a pen and paper and be ready to jot down pertinent information.

★ When attending a meeting. Keep brief notes on who said what; write down detailed notes of issues directly involving you.

* When having phone conversations. Keep notes as you're talking to the other person since you may be unable later to recall accurately what was discussed. Always make sure that you note the caller's contact information in case you have follow-up questions.

* When complaints are made. This is a key protection for you; write down the complaint and how you handled it. Keep notes of follow-up action. These may come in handy if the boss gets involved and wants to know what happened. You will come off as professional and prepared if you can relate what took place from your written notes.

If you're not confident in your ability to take good notes, you should do the following:

* Practice to develop your skill. If you're not a fast writer, come up with some shorthand you will understand, especially for common terms in your business. If you're really slow at taking written notes, practice while watching a news program or listening to talk radio to try to increase your speed. You really will become faster and more accurate over time.

★ Ask questions. If you're not clear as to what someone is saying, you can always comment, "I'm not clear what you mean by that," or ask, "Can you give me an example of what you mean?" Never assume anything. Don't worry about appearing stupid—think how dumb you'll look if you get it wrong.

★ Repeat key points. When the boss is finished telling you something, say "I'd like to read back some of my notes to make sure I've got it correctly." Make sure you verify dates, names, spellings, specific instructions or key objectives.

★ Keep notes organized. Always have a notebook ready to grab and take notes, along with a pen or pencil. Don't try to jot down instructions on loose papers or other materials such as your hand (I've seen people do this, so don't try to deny it). If that happens, immediately transcribe it into your notebook at the first opportunity. Use a notebook that is easy to write in whether you are sitting, standing or walking. Once a notebook is full, write on the front the period of time that it covers—this will make it easy to keep your notes organized.

35. Asking for a Raise You Don't Deserve

Why do you deserve a raise? Some people have what they believe to be perfectly valid reasons:[14]

* ★ "I come to work each day and no one else does."

* ★ "I need more money because I want a car with leather seats."

* ★ "It would be good for morale."

* ★ "I sit at her desk, so I deserve her salary."

Is it any wonder that bosses find it easy to say "No!" to these requests? These people couldn't make it easier to have their bids for more money turned down unless they lobbed a water balloon at the boss's head.

Many companies these days are pretty up front with employees about their financial health. Employees are told that their performance directly impacts the current and future fiscal health of a

[14] Accountemps survey, 1998

company; workers must strive to keep the business competitive in challenging economic times. So, if you're going to ask for more money, then you're going to have to demonstrate that your performance has a positive impact on the company's bottom line. Claiming you need new furniture for your home or want to take a vacation to some exotic locale will not be seen as a legitimate reason for giving you a raise.

Perhaps you believe when you don't get a raise that your boss is just being a tightwad. Not true. Today, many companies don't offer annual cost-of-living raises, but instead reward only top performers with money, stock or other benefits. Just because you are employed doesn't mean you are guaranteed more money every year. Often your boss is in the same boat. She must prove her worth to her bosses in order to merit a pay increase. Can you imagine how your boss would tell her boss that she gave you a raise—not because you're doing a terrific job—but because you want to remodel your kitchen? Such reasoning could cost your boss *her* next raise.

She also may be listening to you ask for a raise and thinking: "Where has this person been living? The land of Oz? Didn't he read our quarterly report and see that our costs are going up? Doesn't he know that I've been up every night for the past two weeks just trying to find money in the budget for a new fax machine? And he wants a raise to buy a new jet ski? How clueless can a person be?"

I know all this sounds discouraging and I don't mean to make you believe your chances of getting a raise are between slim and none. Many companies are committed to rewarding employees who deserve it. Employers are very aware of what the competition is paying, and if they don't want to lose key performers, they know that they're going to have to pony up in order to retain top workers.

What I am saying is that with some guidance you can greatly improve your chances of not only getting the raise you want but of making the boss feel that she can justify it to the top brass. You want to not only make the boss believe that giving you a raise was the smartest thing she's ever done but also make her wonder why she didn't think of it sooner.

When asking for a raise:

* Build your case. Look at how your performance went above and beyond what is expected and how your contributions made a real impact on the success of your department. Be able to cite specific instances of where you made a real difference.

* Get noticed. If you don't have anything that really makes you shine, then now is the time to volunteer for projects that will call attention to your skills.

* Provide documentation. Awards or memos noting a specific contribution are always valuable to share during a salary negotiation.

* Do your homework. Know what others in your field with similar skills and experience are earning.

* Time it right. Make an appointment to speak with the boss—you don't want to try to ask for a raise as she's rushing off to a meeting or bothered by phone calls. Also, don't approach the boss for a raise when you know the company is going through tough times. Pay attention to belt-tightening procedures such as a cutback in business travel, a hiring freeze or no holiday parties.

★ Keep it strictly business. Don't bring personal needs into the discussion, such as the fact that your daughter's private school is raising its tuition or that you're trying to buy a condo.

★ Don't threaten. Saying something like, "If I don't get more money, I'm going to quit" is dumb, dumb, dumb. You've not only backed the boss into a corner but you've clued her into the fact that you're so disloyal you're going to jump ship the first time you don't get your way. Often, threats to quit over money become self-fulfilling—bosses are much more willing to give the boot to employees they believe to be concerned only with their own bottom line.

★ Know when to back off. Don't enter a boss's office determined to get an answer. Give her some time to consider your request. "I'd like you to consider everything I've outlined and perhaps we can discuss it again next week." If you are turned down, then approach the boss again in three or four months. You don't want to nag, but do want to keep your contributions in her sights and under consideration for more money.

Finally, remember to thank your boss right away when you do get your raise. Either do it in person or send a thank-you note. Mention how proud you are to have the job—and getting extra money just makes it even better. This appreciation and acknowledgment of the boss's action will not only keep you in a positive light but will also lay the groundwork for future rewards and recognition.

36. Lacking Knowledge of Current Events

Dear Anita,

I was asked to attend a lunch with my boss and some clients. While we were waiting for our food, the conversation at the table turned to a recent kidnapping overseas of some important U.S. diplomat. I had no idea what they were talking about, and I thought it was kind of rude that they would discuss something that I obviously didn't know (or care) about. I sort of hinted to my boss later that I didn't think it was very polite and he looked at me really weird. But, Anita, don't you think it was rude and that I had every right to expect good manners from these people? Just because I don't earn as much money as they do doesn't give them the right to act like I don't matter!

Miffed Martha

Dear Martha,

Could it possibly be that the boss was looking at you "really weird" because he wondered if perhaps you lived under a

rock? Businesses are impacted greatly by daily world events, and your ignorance has the boss worried that you really don't know (or care) about anything outside your cubicle.
Anita

I n my research for this chapter, I found an article from a Canadian university about one of its professors who decided to test his students' understanding of terms often used in daily headlines. Specifically, students were asked about words and phrases such as catch-22, Big Brother, placebo, jihad, blitzkrieg and spin doctor.

The story said that the professor found that many students didn't understand the words. And while that may not sound too momentous, the professor admitted in the article that he was concerned.

"People are less likely to read a news story if they don't understand the headline," noted Dr. Sheldon Ungar. "Ignorance of many common phrases isn't just a statement of what people know, it is an indicator of what people are likely to learn. This ignorance has consequences."

Consequences that worry your boss.

In today's fast-paced marketplace, bosses depend greatly on an employee's ability to grow and to change as needed, and part of this ability comes from understanding the bigger picture. If an employee can't grasp important world events and stay current on developments, the boss will worry the employee simply has limited learning capacity.

Further, if the boss is going to give you a leadership role then he's got to feel confident that you can handle yourself intelligently in a variety of situations—and being oblivious to current events may mean you will embarrass not only yourself but the boss as well. Let's say, for example, you're just shooting the breeze a bit before a meeting with a customer. The customer mentions how the tax debate in the state legislature is likely to affect his ability to operate next year. The customer looks to you for your input. But you can't think of a thing to say, since you have no idea what he's talking about. What tax debate? The last time you looked at a newspaper you only read *Dilbert*. And you never watch the local news—too boring!

Your lack of input into this conversation may be puzzling, at best. But the worst-case scenario is that the customer loses some respect for you, and for your boss and your company. Does the customer really want to do business with a company where the employees are unaware of vital events affecting his business?

In 1964, 81 percent of Americans read a daily newspaper while only 54 percent do so today.[15] Millions of people surf the Internet every day but the sites they visit may have absolutely nothing to do with current events—only 11 percent of young people say it's a major source of news. The three nightly news programs have seen their ratings plunge 44 percent since 1980.

Corporate leaders also are concerned about the image of "the ugly American"—the person who is ignorant of world events and has little or no interest in what goes on outside of the United States. Since many employers do business globally—or at least make money from international visitors to this country—providing an image of being educated and aware of the world is important.

"Corporations today are subjected more than ever to the factors going on around the world, and what's happening economically and politically globally affects all of us," says Corinne L.

[15] Evan Cornog, *Columbia Journalism Review*, Jan./Feb. 2005

Gediman, an adult learning specialist and corporate trainer. "People will never advance in their careers if they don't understand the link between business and world issues."

That's why when you can demonstrate to your boss that you not only know who is the chief justice of the United States but can speak intelligently about the city council's next election, then you've just risen a notch in the boss's eyes. The boss understands that if you can grasp these concepts and speak about them thoughtfully, then you would be capable of leading a team discussion on plans for the next business quarter or spearheading a project that requires maturity and common sense. He knows that you're unlikely to embarrass him with your naiveté or ignorance in front of customers or his boss.

I'll admit that I'm a news junkie, which makes sense since I'm a journalist. And I gotta tell you—I cringe when I hear someone say, "I don't watch or read the news—it's too depressing." Believe me, I often find it depressing and I understand that all news all the time can be overwhelming. I'm not saying you should do nothing but immerse yourself in the news, but I am saying that there's no excuse for not being aware of what is going on in the world. If you can't grasp what is going on in the world around you, then you really limit yourself on the job.

"Because of the pace of change in the world today, skill sets and knowledge become old quickly. Workers need to remain mentally agile and if they don't do it on the most basic level—such as keeping up with current events—then they're going to have difficulty keeping up in their careers," Gediman says.

Understanding and digesting what is happening in the world gives context and meaning to your life, and that certainly includes your job. Let's say you work for a hotel in a popular tourist destination. With oil-producing nations limiting their oil supply to this country, your employer may be greatly impacted when visitors can no longer afford vacations via car or plane because gas prices are so high. Because you understand that what is happening halfway across the world can directly impact your employer, you begin to brainstorm with managers to come up with other ways to make revenue for your company.

Your boss now sees you as someone who is sharp enough to see the big picture, and the impact it can have—and that's the kind of employee who gets ahead on the job.

To be seen in the eyes of the boss and others as clued in and on top of what is happening in the world around you, make sure you cover your the bases. That means you need to take some steps:

★ Tune in. Don't claim you don't have time to pay attention to the news. I don't buy it and neither does your boss. Spend at least ten minutes a day learning of the top news stories—you can watch the twenty-four-hour television news shows while getting dressed for work or listen to one on the radio. Read the newspaper while eating breakfast. Try to watch ten or fifteen minutes of a morning show to catch up on the latest trends, or read the feature section of a newspaper, noting the latest celebrity or trend news. Try not to get your news from only one source: Different views can be put on events and you want to make sure you hear the facts, not just the "spin."

★ Scan the headlines every morning. If you don't want to buy a newspaper, go online to one of the national media sites, such as *USA Today* (www.usatoday.com), *The New York Times* (www.nytimes.com) or CNN (www.cnn.com). This way you'll have a general idea about the top stories of the day.

★ Go in-depth. At least once a week, find a news magazine or television or radio show that will provide a deeper look at an issue. Try to challenge yourself and learn about a subject that is unfamiliar to you.

★ Join in. Don't sit back and let the world pass you by. Join a civic cause or volunteer at community activities. This will help you become familiar with important issues in your area.

★ Make it enjoyable. If you are living away from your hometown, read its news online or subscribe to its local newspaper. That way, you can keep up on hometown news and learn a thing or two about the rest of the world. Watch some of the late-night shows to get a laugh while staying informed of the day's happenings.

Remember that while the news can sometimes be pretty grim, it can also be fun, exciting and informative. So, whether you're learning about the global trade conference, the latest celebrity gossip or how to grow strawberries, don't miss the opportunity to learn more about the world around you. That kind of knowledge will pay off at work and in the rest of your life.

37. Holding Grudges

Maybe you're still a little mad at the coworker who didn't back you up in a meeting even though he promised he would. Perhaps you're still hurt that someone you trained got the promotion you wanted. Or, you're sick and tired of always covering the phones for a coworker who takes a long lunch every day.

If you're holding a grudge for a perceived injustice at work, either big or small, then you're stuck. Your feelings keep you from giving 100 percent to the job. For example, you don't want to help solve a problem because the person you trained—and who got the job you wanted—is involved. "Just let her try to figure it out if she's so special," you think.

Or, the guy who didn't back you in a meeting is swamped with work and looking for help. You certainly do not feel the least inclined to help him even though his backlog will affect an entire department. "Let the disloyal jerk fend for himself," you think. "Then he'll know how it feels."

Sort of like digging through the trash, isn't it? It's a dirty, nasty habit that the boss wants you to stop. Why? The boss doesn't want someone holding onto garbage that will impact the efficiency and productivity of an operation. Your ability to move past it and get on with the task at hand is what matters to him—he wants your energy focused on the job and not on past grievances.

So, it's time to do a little housekeeping and give up the grudges. You need to do the following:

* Live in the real world. You cannot rewrite history. You cannot go back and change the fact that your coworker didn't back you up in the meeting. You can't change the fact that you didn't get the promotion. Those are done deals. By holding on to your grudge, you are telling yourself that you can change those moments of your life. You can't.

* Hold yourself accountable. Maybe you think you're angry with someone else when, in fact, you're mad at yourself. You're mad at your coworker not because he didn't back you up, but because you put your fate in his hands. If you'd been better prepared, you could have performed better. You're not angry because you have to answer the phone at lunch, but because you keep postponing talking with the coworker about the problem.

* Put it in perspective. Sometimes we obsess over truly silly things. We can get so caught up in being mad because Sue and Tom took a long coffee break that we miss the fact that Bill is upset because his mom is terminally ill. When you feel your anger and resentment start to build, take the time to look at the world around you and put things in perspective.

★ Find other outlets. Even the nicest rats in the world can get mad at each other if scientists put enough of them in a confined space. When you're away from work, find physical outlets to release your garbage—whack a ball, pound a bag or just walk. Keep a journal (not online!—see #8) to help you vent your feelings.

38. Giving Lackluster Speeches or Presentations

On an early morning local television news program a couple of years ago, a female anchor began interviewing a young man about an upcoming event. He managed to answer the first question with little trouble, but when the next question came, he swallowed heavily before he could answer. The anchor continued, but the guy became paler by the moment. As he attempted to answer the next question, he puked all over the anchor desk. The startled newswoman looked at the camera and gamely said, "I think we'll take a short break."

The young man survived, of course, although many of us might consider dying on the spot from the embarrassment. He did, in fact, achieve some level of notoriety when the video was used on several blooper programs. It just goes to prove that you can survive even the worst imaginable public-speaking debacle and live to tell about it.

Some people get more nervous than others when speaking in front of others, becoming a sweating, shaking bundle of hyperventilating nerves when confronted with a podium and a microphone.

Some research suggests that those who flounder severely when asked to give a presentation or speech have had some early childhood trauma or phobia.

Since that's not my area of expertise, I want to focus instead on fine-tuning your speaking abilities.

Being asked to make a presentation or give a speech is not a punishment—it is an honor. It is a recognition that others are impressed enough with your skills and abilities that they want to learn from you. In this day and age of electronic communication, it truly is something special when people will gather in person to hear your words.

The secret, experts say, is that anyone giving a speech or presentation—no matter the size of the audience—needs to be prepared. It's important to remember that often those in a business audience can help make or break a career and your performance serves as a direct reflection on your boss. Come off as a stumbling, bumbling idiot and folks will wonder what the boss was thinking when he hired you. Put on a good, solid presentation or speech and your boss and others will begin to see you in a new light—as a leader capable of influencing others and commanding respect.

What makes a good presentation or speech? One of the keys is making sure you understand your audience and what is expected from you.

In a presentation, for example, the audience often participates by asking questions. In order to give an effective presentation, you need to do several things:

★ Set the agenda. Explain to the group what you'll be doing and when they can ask questions.

★ Manage the time. Have a small watch handy so you can easily see that your presentation is running according to schedule. If you see that one issue is taking too long with one person, offer to meet afterwards to discuss it further. You don't want others in the group to become bored and restless. Only answer one question per person.

★ Keep answers short and to the point. Don't get involved in offering a complete history of a project or you'll quickly bore the people who didn't have the question. Give one fact to support your answer and move on.

★ Plant "friendlies." If you're concerned about giving the presentation, ask a few friendly colleagues to ask questions that you've written out for them beforehand. Request they stick to the question and not try to alter it in any way or you could be in for an unwelcome surprise when you don't know the answer.

★ Watch body language. Keep an eye on your group. An advantage to a presentation is that the group is often smaller, which can allow you to monitor their reaction. If you believe they're becoming bored, move along quickly. If it appears they are confused or skeptical, use it as an opportunity to solicit comments or questions.

★ Keep your cool. In a smaller group, anger or resentment will become quickly apparent. Don't get defensive if you're asked a tough question. Give yourself time by repeating or paraphrasing the query, then giving a point to support your answer, followed by a brief explanation. If you don't know the answer say, "That's interesting. We're collecting information on that, and I'll get back to you later with what we find out."

* Summarize with impact. At the end, don't just gather all your materials and say, "Well, if there are no more questions, that's it." Give a statement and plan of action: "By using this new system, we'll drive this company into higher profitability while infusing our employees with a new commitment to quality and efficiency. It's going to be a remarkable and exciting time for all of us and training in your departments is our start-up bell."

If you're asked to give a speech, use the first minute to tell a (clean) joke, a story that involves you or something else that will grab their attention such as some interesting fact. Then, you need to continue with the following:

* Provide a roadmap. Let the audience know from the get-go why you're standing in front of them. "I'm here today to talk about . . ." Then immediately let them know where you stand by saying something like, "I believe we can create a more efficient operation by . . ." Most people don't like getting in a car with someone who doesn't know where the heck he or she is going, and audience members often don't like being subjected to a freewheeling speaker. Let them know why you've been chosen to speak to them, why the employer is interested in the topic and why it is of interest to the audience. This helps the audience relax and take in your

viewpoints—you've proven you know what you're talking about and they're in good hands.

* Focus on substance. Some people spend too much time trying to create a dynamite beginning, looking for a pithy comment worthy of Thomas Jefferson or a joke that would be coveted by Jay Leno. However, the audience is attending the speech to hear what *you* know, so focus more on the crux of the speech. The beginning and ending will come much easier, in fact, when you've got the heart of the speech completed.

* Avoid numbers. Peppering your speech with statistics may look good on paper, but people have a hard time grasping the significance of such facts when given to them verbally. "Numbers are easy to use, but they're the worst thing you can do," says Mark Wiskup, a communications expert and a former television journalist. "Numbers are meaningless. Look at it this way: The richest, most meaningful conversations don't involve numbers. You don't say to your child, 'I loved you six times today.' You give people numbers, and you disconnect them."

* Look for friendlies. Unlike the presentation, you may not be able to plant people you know in the audience. But don't panic—there are usually people in an audience who look directly at you, often smiling or nodding. These are the people you need to look at when you get nervous, or just to give you confidence. Let your eyes skip over the guy using his BlackBerry or the woman fixing her lipstick.

* Let them down gently. At the conclusion, don't abruptly walk away when you're done or ramble on about nothing for ten minutes. The conclusion should take about a minute and can be a brief summarization of your speech, or a short story.

Practice your speech or presentation until you feel comfortable enough with the information that you won't stumble and freeze if you can't read it verbatim. You should try to practice in front of friends or family members to get their feedback, or use a video recorder to tape your performance to make sure you have a relaxed but professional style. You also can tape-record your voice to see if you use enough inflection and emphasis to make your voice interesting and not sleep-inducing. Another good idea is to show up early at the location to get a feel for the room where you'll be speaking. Remember to avoid using audio or visual equipment that you haven't practiced with or props that you are not comfortable using.

If you still believe you might need a little polish, try Toastmasters International (www.toastmasters.org), which focuses on helping people to hone their speaking and presentation skills.

Finally, try to relax and enjoy giving your speech and presentation. It is, after all, a pat on the back for your hard work. Now is the time to feel good about what you've accomplished and look forward to more opportunities to prove your leadership capabilities to the boss.

Part Five

Sis, Boom, Bah! Failure to Give Full Support to Your Employer Says You're Not Ready for an Investment of Time and Resources

We humans can be a stubborn lot. From the time we're old enough to talk we say "No!" to taking naps or eating brussels sprouts. When we're school age, we balk at doing homework. As teenagers, we rebel against everything and everyone. As young adults, we envision forging our own future, committed to doing what we think is right for us.

But in the working world, we're continually doing things we don't necessarily like or want to do. We have to attend business functions that last so long our clothes go out of style. We listen to people who bore us silly or make us so annoyed we'd like to smack them with a rolled-up newspaper. We feign enthusiasm for change when all we'd really like to do is throw a chair through a window or sob like babies.

So, when things don't go our way, we find ways of dealing with it.

We avoid. "Oops—I forgot!" we exclaim in mock chagrin as we are informed we missed the company-sponsored fund-raiser for a local charity.

We dodge. "Oh? The seminar? Yes . . . it was productive for me," you say, remembering the holiday shopping you managed to get done by ditching a couple of sessions.

We play innocent. "Why, of *course* I didn't notice the new employee was confused and couldn't get the hang of things! I've just been so busy! I thought when he locked himself in the supply closet for hours he just wanted some alone time!"

Tsk, tsk. Such shenanigans. You really don't fool anyone with these antics, you know. Those tactics have been around since the snake said, "Who, me?" in the Garden of Eden and Milli Vanilli exclaimed, "What's lip-synching?"

One of the biggest areas of concern for any boss is making sure his bosses don't think he's wasting time or resources. Many smaller businesses operate pretty close to the bone, so they don't have dollars to waste. Even bigger companies with a larger profit margin make their managers report down to the penny what they've done with allocated resources.

So, let's say the boss asks you to attend a seminar. When you return he asks you what you learned, and you sort of hem and haw. After all, the speakers were boring and most of the subjects didn't interest you. You manage to put together a so-so report for the boss but don't even attempt to use any of the information in your everyday activities at work. But here's what the boss is thinking: "I gave the employee a paid absence to attend the seminar and footed the bill for attendance fees and travel expenses—and now there's nothing but this mediocre report to show for it!"

Exactly how do you think your boss will feel when he has to explain this very limited return on investment to his boss?

And that's the key here: Your boss must answer to his boss. Anything you do, or don't do, reflects directly on your boss. He must explain to his boss why you wasted money, or why your performance is not contributing to the bottom line. You may think that by showing up for work every day that you do contribute to a company's profit, but that's not necessarily true. As I've mentioned before, an increasingly complex and competitive global marketplace means that every company—every employee—must go that extra mile in order to survive.

Let's consider another scenario of how limited support from you impacts your boss and your company. A new directive has come from corporate headquarters, and the boss says there will be some new goals this year. You roll your eyes when you hear this, earning a snicker or two from colleagues. After the boss explains the plan, you huddle with other coworkers at lunch. You make disparaging comments about the changes, even calling the boss a few unflattering names at the same time. In the coming weeks, you conveniently "forget" to implement some of the changes, and the ones you do practice are done halfheartedly.

You notice the boss, meanwhile, is under continuing stress to get the changes implemented, but you just sort of mentally shrug your shoulders. That's his problem, you think.

Wrong. If the boss has a problem, then it's your problem. If he cares about it, then you should too. If he's looking for a solution, then you better help find it.

Why? Because if things don't go well, you can count on blame being passed around. Your boss is going to get some of it, but you better believe he's going to be looking for someone to share it—and that would be you. The person who made snide comments, who didn't commit 100 percent to making the changes successful and certainly didn't give 110 percent.

Depending on the boss, the repercussions may be that you are not given the days off you wanted to compete in a marathon, or you are not considered for the next promotion. Or, a plum job opens up in another department but the boss feels no compunction whatsoever to put in a good word for you. Bosses know other bosses. They hang out with other bosses, they share horror stories with other bosses and they watch out for one another. They may not dis you outright to another boss, but they'll make it clear that you're not someone who's willing to put in any extra effort on the job, and may be disloyal to boot. (Always count on your unflattering words about the company or the boss to eventually make their way back to the boss.)

The point is that if you want the boss to put in a good word for you when it's needed, if you want him to invest some time and resources in things that interest you, or if you'd just like to benefit from who and what he knows, then you're going to have to be a little more enthusiastic about supporting him and your company.

In other words, you need to be a cheerleader for your boss and your company. This doesn't mean you go overboard and do backflips every time the boss makes a move. But it does mean that you offer support, encouragement and maybe even a few high fives when things are going well. It means that when things are not going well, you remain supportive with comments focusing on the future and what can be achieved.

What else do you need to do? You find ways to partner with the boss, to offer him your skills and talents to help him achieve his goals. You become a loyal team player, refusing to slam corporate goals or insult him to others. You stay dependable, becoming the person who is willing to pitch in and help a new employee learn the ropes, or offer your willingness and enthusiasm whenever and wherever it's needed. You don't demand recognition, but earn it by being a smart and professional employee who understands company goals and is committed to meeting them.

None of this is hard, but it does take maturity and a personal resolve to step up and help out when others may not. It takes a real commitment to keeping your eye on what is important to the boss, to constantly adjusting your inner radar to know what matters in a shifting marketplace that continually makes new demands. But once you've adapted to being flexible and open to new challenges, then you've put yourself in a position of being highly valuable to the boss—and that's just the place you want to be.

39. Squandering Time at Seminars

Dear Anita,

My significant other got mad at me when I went deep-sea fishing without him, because it's something he has always wanted to do. I explained that I only went because the company was paying for it. Well, not exactly the fishing, but my employer did pay for me to attend the seminar that was near this great fishing spot. I told him that the seminar was a huge waste of my time and at least I salvaged the trip with the fishing thing. Do you think it would be un-professional for me to take my significant other with me on my next business trip so that he won't feel so left out?

Bonnie Voyage

Dear Bonnie,

The minute you put that lure in the water you did your em-ployer a disservice. You could have been networking with business associates, lining up future deals or even finding new resources for colleagues who were working while you

were playing with Flipper. I'll bet your sweetie isn't the only
one who doesn't appreciate your actions.

Anita

Attending a seminar or convention is often like preparing for
battle. You approach it armed with all the necessary equipment
you require to stay alive for hours, days, weeks. Laptop, cell
phone, pager, notebooks, business cards, briefcase, Blackberry, the
daily newspaper, iPod, coffee, pens, pencils, coat, unopened mail
and a change of shoes. And, of course, a little postlunch pick-me-
up in the form of an extra-large chocolate bar. (It's always best to
be prepared for a long day.)

OK, you're rarin' to go. Ready to settle in and learn something
so riveting it should be on *Montel*. You're ready to focus on the
speaker and the presentation. But first, you decide to check your
messages on e-mail and voice mail. Once that's done, you're ready
to settle down and listen. Then your eye catches the day's headlines. A baseball strike? What? You read the entire article before
you realize others around you are taking notes on whatever the
heck the speaker is saying. You hurriedly paw through your briefcase, trying to find your notebook and a pen. Oops . . . pen doesn't
work. OK, now you're ready with a pencil and pad.

After the session, you decide to stroll through the exhibition
hall, gathering little goodies as you go. A tennis ball for the dog,
some M&M's for sustenance (the chocolate bar is long gone and
it's not even lunchtime), markers, a travel mug and a key ring. A
professional acquaintance approaches, introducing you to a colleague. You try to juggle all the stuff in your hands but drop the
markers and the tennis ball, which rolls under an exhibitor's table.
After a bit of scrambling, you offer a handshake to the new busi-

ness contact—only to discover your hand is smeared with melted chocolate.

Once the convention is over, you haul all your stuff out of the meeting room, grab a cab and head to the airport. But as you fumble for your driver's license in the airport terminal, some receipts you had stuffed in your coat pocket drop out. You think you got them all crammed back in your briefcase, but you can't be sure because your briefcase is packed to the brim with meeting materials and you may have dropped some of those as you were running to make your plane.

The next day you're back in the office and the boss stops by your desk. "How was the seminar?" she asks.

"Terrific!" you answer. "Brought back good information and some new contacts!"

"Great," the boss says. "I'd like to see a report next week on what you think might be worthwhile to share with others and you can submit your expense report as soon as you have it ready."

The boss leaves, and you begin unloading your briefcase. Funny, but you thought you had more materials, and whatever happened to all those meal receipts? And you just know you had several business cards from valuable contacts—now you only have one. But wait! At the bottom of your bag you can feel something—must either be the receipts or the cards. When you pull it out, it is neither.

It is a used chocolate bar wrapper with a smashed M&M attached.

Sigh.

Seminars and conventions can be terrific, but let's face it: They also can be a big pain in the butt. We have to lug all our stuff around, we may have to put up with boring speakers and *why, oh why* does the temperature in the meeting rooms have to be a sweltering eighty-five or a nippy fifty degrees?

It's tempting to blow off at least some of a convention or a seminar. So, we do a little shopping or sightseeing instead, believing we deserve a little R&R because we work so hard. Or, we try to do too many other things while attending a session—we read mail, check messages, jot down notes for a future meeting or read celebrity gossip in the newspaper.

Any or all of those actions aren't horrible—they're just not in keeping with the spirit of why you were sent in the first place. The boss sent you to the convention to learn something. If you don't learn anything from a specific session, then you should be able to learn something from the other attendees—colleagues, vendors and experts can catch you up on the latest news and trends in your industry. If you're unorganized or distracted taking care of other business, then you're squandering the boss's investment in you.

"If you're not paying attention, or even if some of this stuff is boring to you, you can still come up with a report on what happened that might be useful to someone else you work with," says Kate Wendleton, founder of a career coaching and outplacement firm. "You can get such a wealth of information at these things: what the competition is doing; the challenges others are facing and how they are overcoming them; or what strategies they're planning to implement."

That's why it's important that you prepare for a seminar or convention so that you and your boss get the most return on the investment of time and resources. You should do the following:

* Plan ahead. Before you attend a seminar, read the materials sent by the group sponsoring the event. Highlight sessions you would like to attend, looking for potential time con-

flicts. You might be able to receive audiotapes of sessions you can't attend, or perhaps you can agree with a colleague beforehand to attend different sessions, exchanging information later. The key is to have specific objectives in mind when attending an event, such as meeting certain people or getting information on new products. Make sure your days are planned around those objectives.

* Pack appropriately. You're not going to the convention to catch up on work or be hooked to your e-mail or voice mail. While you can set up an office in your hotel room, don't try to do other work while attending a session. Try to keep your supplies to a minimum, with a couple of folders that will allow you to file information immediately. One folder will be for items that need immediate action, while another may be for filing when you get home. Don't be afraid to pitch useless items in the trash can—it's just one less thing for you to lug around. At the same time, bring some pre-addressed heavy-duty envelopes to the convention so you can mail home materials that you won't immediately need.

* Organize your cards. It's always easiest to exchange business cards if you have them in a pocket. Trying to find them in a purse or a briefcase can resemble a Jerry Lewis routine and takes the focus away from the contact. After you receive a card, jot notes on it to help you remember key points; don't hesitate to throw away cards that you know will be of no use to you.

* Stay organized. Receipts often are difficult to keep track of when you're traveling. Fold in the flap of an envelope and

keep it in your bag, then simply put receipts inside as you receive them. This also will make it easy to retrieve them and do your expense report as you travel home.

★ Review your efforts. When you get home, think about what you liked and didn't like about the particular seminar. Jot down notes for next year on what you would do differently and what worked well for you. The boss will appreciate knowing if company money is being wisely spent on this venture, or if another convention or seminar would be worth the employer's investment of time and resources.

40. Skipping Company-Sponsored Events

Most companies have at least one or more events a year that bring everyone together outside of work. Usually there is the annual holiday party or summer picnic, and sometimes a company will be involved in a charity or community event, helping to underwrite some—or all—of the cost.

The majority of employees usually attend such events if for no reason other than to take advantage of free food and drink. It's also a chance for many employees to introduce family and friends to work associates and to the boss—and for the family and friends to take advantage of free food and drink.

Still, there are some people who have no intention of attending a company-sponsored event unless a subpoena is involved.

Some employees feel that they spend enough time with co-workers and the boss during regular working hours and that they shouldn't have to spend even twenty minutes at a company event. So what if the employer is footing the bill for a charity event or trying to establish stronger community ties? Too bad. These workers believe they put in their time at work, get paid for it, and then should be free to do whatever they want. That's certainly true. No one should be made to attend a company-sponsored event.

But let's look at it from another perspective for a moment. What if this event could not only help get you a raise, but perhaps a promotion? Would you attend if the boss said: "Help with the marathon run for the local hospital and I'll give you $3,000 and a new office"?

OK, that might be pushing the envelope a bit, but it's certainly not out of the realm of possibility. The point is that being seen as someone who is supportive of company efforts after hours can boost your standing not only with your boss, but also with the boss's boss. That's invaluable stuff. It's not every day that you are given a chance to rub elbows with other company brass (besides your direct supervisor), and to do so at an event where the atmosphere is likely to be more relaxed and genial than during regular business hours. Chatting with the boss's boss in such a setting automatically casts you in a positive light because you're seen as being supportive of your employer and its efforts.

Further, your presence at such a charity event championed by your employer helps the company to foster a positive community impression.

"There are some companies that won't do business with other businesses that are not seen as having corporate social responsibility," says Kate Wendleton, founder of a career coaching and outplacement company. "That's why it's very important to bosses that you're seen as putting a positive face on for the community."

Your visible support of the employer makes the boss much more willing, therefore, to invest her energies and resources in you. In other words, she sees you going above and beyond the call of duty by showing up at the event, so she is willing to do the same for your career.

At the same time, a boss who notices you can't be bothered to show up at a company event likely will be less willing to put any extra effort into your career aspirations. Bosses, after all, may be embarrassed in front of their bosses if few employees show up to events or functions that the company underwrites.

Still, it's not all about the boss. There are other benefits to attending company-sponsored events. Many times, friends and family attend events such as picnics or parties, and meeting them can help you establish better relationships with coworkers. For example, let's say you've had trouble connecting with a coworker who seems very reserved and often critical of your work efforts. But upon meeting his wife, you discover that he has a great love of woodworking. You also love the craft and find that discussions about it help break the ice with him. Further, you learn from the family member that he suffers from a chronic illness, which is why he is sometimes cranky and critical. In the future, you know you'll be more aware of those times he isn't feeling well and show some extra patience.

Another added benefit for your career in attending a company event is that it gives you a chance to network with others in the community. Just think how appreciative the boss will be if you mention a new customer you garnered through a company event, or the philanthropic leader you met who offered to set up a meeting with a potential company investor.

Now that you can see that attending such events is worthwhile for many reasons, what's the best way to have them pay off for you? You should keep the following in mind:

⋆ Be prepared. What do you talk about when you're standing right next to the CEO at a party? It helps if you can make some polite small talk, but it also is a chance to show you're a valuable member of the company. "When the big boss asks you how you're doing, don't just say, 'fine,'" Wendleton says. "Say something like, 'Oh, I'm doing so great. I've been working really hard, and I've come up with this great new idea.' And the boss says, 'Really? I didn't know that. Tell me about it.'" It's rare that you'll get a chance to be within arm's reach of some top brass; don't waste the opportunity to shine.

★ Listen and learn. Don't immediately stick your business card in someone's face at a community or charity event. The atmosphere is more relaxed—take some time to learn a few things about the person. "What brings you to this event?" you can ask. "Is this your first time?" When initially meeting someone, try to say the name immediately to help you remember his or her name. "It's nice to meet you, Tom." Then, if you chat about business and it appears this person might be good to contact again, supply a business card. "It was nice speaking with you and learning about your job. Enjoy the rest of the event," you say when it's time to go.

★ Move beyond your comfort zone. At many company-sponsored events, employees who already know one another seem to cluster together like a bunch of hens before a storm. These situations are the perfect opportunity to approach people you don't know and introduce yourself. People are feeling much more sociable and accommodating away from work, and your common purpose in attending (raising money for a hospital, etc.) bond you together in a unique way. I once worked at a local food bank for a couple of hours, and while bagging potatoes I found myself getting to know three local business leaders quite well. (Being covered in dirt and squashing potato bugs together seemed to really bond us.)

★ Mind your manners. While working in the hot summer sun to build a house or freezing your buns off while helping with a holiday parade can cause you to lose more than a few inhibitions, don't forget who you represent when you are at a company-supported event. You become the face and name of your company. Make yourself the best representative you can by being polite and respectful of others.

★ Remember it's not about you. When you attend a company event, don't bitch about the food, whine about coworkers or complain that you'd rather be playing golf. Put on your happy face and stop acting like a thirteen-year-old who just got braces. Your own personal nirvana does not matter at this moment. You should be seen as being supportive of the employer and the event.

41. Ignoring the Company's Goals

It's easy to get a case of chronic job complaining. You grumble and gripe about what you do and what you don't get to do. You never seem to be happy—you don't get paid enough, you don't have the title you want and you don't get the respect you believe you deserve.

Part of the problem with chronic complaining is that you focus on fixing the blame, not the problem. It's the boss's fault that you're not getting a raise. It's a coworker's fault that you didn't get a promotion. And it's definitely someone else's fault that you've gotten a reputation as being a whiny grump.

But is it really? Is someone really at fault or is it your own actions—and inactions—that are the real problem?

Let me ask you this: What is your employer's number one goal? If you answer anything besides "making money," you go to the back of the class. Your company is in business to make money, which you should be very happy about because if it didn't you (a) probably would not have a job, and (b) probably would not get paid. OK, now the next question: What are the top goals for your employer (after making money) this year?

And the final question is: Do you even *want* to know what the goals are?

You should know and you should care. Why? Because these are what you will tie your own career goals to. If you don't, success at work may elude you. Let me stress that I'm not saying you should abandon all your lifetime personal career aspirations. I'm just pointing out that if you want a boss to sit up and take notice, then you're going to have to show him how simpatico your goals are. The boss will appreciate the employee who makes that connection—and become uneasy with the worker who doesn't.

Judith Glaser, CEO of a communications strategy company, says those who have an "I don't care attitude" about their employer's goals pass on that attitude to others. That "sense of ennui" becomes a "toxic disease" in the workplace, she says.

That said, do you think your boss will want to let the source of that infection hang around? Or will he seek to eradicate the employee who drags others down, refusing to focus on company goals?

If you want to get yourself out of such a situation, let's consider some of the tactics you can use to keep focused on goals that will help not only your company but your own career:

★ Get into the boss's head. The boss's goals are tightly connected to his boss, and on up the line. That means that if the boss cares about terrific customer service and has implemented several new rules for dealing with customers, you can bet it's because the word came from much higher up. The boss knows his raise or promotion depends on it so you should have the same strategy. Focus on how you can come up with strategies to support the boss's efforts, and then make sure he is aware of your efforts. Try to use the same language as the boss when discussing these plans—that makes it even easier for him to understand where your focus is and he will be more likely to remember you for rewards and recognition.

★ Do it better. If one of the company's goals is to be more competitive, find ways to improve a process or operate more efficiently. Trimming inefficient practices to make the operation function smoother can certainly be seen as helping the employer to operate more competitively. The point is to try to work company goals into your everyday activities on the job. Make sure you document your efforts and the results so that when performance evaluations roll around, you have concrete proof of your efforts to meet company goals.

★ Ask questions. When you consider an action or an idea, ask yourself questions such as, "How does this meet company goals?" "Will this pay off in the long term for the company, or will it only have a short-term impact that won't really be worth it?" "Is this the best use of my time for attaining the company objectives?" Always ask yourself or others involved whether some alternatives are available that might better meet the employer goals.

★ Pick up the dropped ball. Nothing drives a boss bonkers quicker than seeing a project or effort simply abandoned. By stepping in and offering your skills and abilities, you're telling the boss: "This is important to the company and to you, so it's important to me."

If you'd like to gain more insight about trends and issues that concern management in your industry, check out the Society for Human Resource Management's website at www.shrm.org.

42. Dodging Meetings

Workplace meetings often are not very exciting. They often are stressful and they often are too long. But it's important to remember that meetings also are important as much for what is said, as for what is *not* said. In a meeting, you have a chance to closely observe colleagues and bosses—it's a real opportunity to watch and learn and listen.

For example, you can observe who sits together, who supports whom and who uses the gathering as a chance to launch a few verbal missiles. In meetings you can learn of new alliances and of broken ones, and discover who has the real influence (this is usually the person everyone looks at when it's time for a decision to be made).

Meetings also are a good chance to sort of strut your stuff. It's a chance to offer information that will prove valuable to others, an opportunity to show that you're on top of your game and have skills and abilities that make you a force to be reckoned with. Meetings also give you the chance to impress your boss or support her if she needs it.

How can you make sure that you get the most out of any meeting? Here are some dos and don'ts:

★ DO be prepared. Always have a notebook handy to grab for meetings, even a last-minute one. Have a small calendar attached to the notebook as well as an extra pen or pencil.

★ DON'T take the cell phone or pager. If you can't seem to detach them from your body (some people can't), at least turn the thing off.

★ DO sit next to someone different each time. It's not a junior high cafeteria where you will just *die* if you can't sit next to your buddies. Nothing looks sillier than acting as if you'll get cooties by sitting next to someone you don't know well or like.

★ DON'T keep watching the clock. If you can't be discreet about checking your watch, take it off and place it on the table in front of you so at least you won't be so obvious about looking at the time.

★ DO watch your body language. Sitting with your arms crossed tightly, tapping your toe, fiddling with your hair or twirling your pen sends the message that you'd rather be somewhere else. *Everyone* would rather be somewhere else, but it's not good form to broadcast it. Remember, you're in the meeting to watch and to learn, so use your time to advantage. If you think things are getting off track, ask a question to bring the subject back into focus.

★ DO try to participate. If you know of the meeting in advance, try to get an agenda or at least an idea of what will be discussed so you can offer something during the meeting. Usually executive assistants or secretaries will have a more detailed idea of what will be discussed; try to learn as much as you can so you can offer specific ideas or information. If you don't have anything to offer, at least keep eye contact with those who are speaking and take notes.

★ DON'T be shy. If you believe meetings are too long or too boring, then why not volunteer to be in charge of the next one? That way, you have something to keep you occupied during the meeting and you can implement your ideas for a more productive session. It also helps others see you as a "take charge" person.

★ DON'T be late. If you have trouble making it on time, set the meeting time earlier on your calendar so that you will be "fooled" into being on time. It's always better to show up early and spend the time reviewing materials than to show up late.

While it's certainly true that meetings can be frustrating and stressful, it's also true that they are still the best way to exchange ideas, to challenge one another and to get the creative juices flowing. No e-mail or telephone call can beat the face-to-face meeting of opinions and ideas, and that's something none of us should ever be willing to give up.

43. Not Going Beyond Your Job Description

Stepping outside the job description is more important than ever these days. Companies are under enormous pressure to compete globally and bosses don't have time to grill every employee on every skill he or she has. They rely on employees to be smart enough and savvy enough to know what skills they possess and how those abilities can be used to help the bottom line. As organizations "flatten out," bosses are under more pressure than ever before to make sure the teams they develop are running at full speed—and that means there is no time for bellyaching from workers who don't want to step outside the lines.

Think about all your abilities. Can you speak Spanish or read Chinese? Do you know how to use the Internet to track down obscure records or find delinquent customers? These abilities can be used to make yourself more valuable to your employer. While they may not be in a formal job description, bringing all your skills and abilities to an employer will benefit not only the company but yourself.

Still, maybe you just don't feel like telling the boss you speak German and couldn't care less that he has to spend hundreds of dollars having an interpreter come into work for one day to help with a German-speaking customer. But consider this: Do you think he will appreciate your keeping mum about your language skills? Or will he look at you and think, "OK, you don't want to put out any extra effort to help me, so I won't put out any extra effort to help you."

Not sure how to become more valuable? Let's consider some ways you can begin adding more value to your job:

* Be a cheerleader. When somebody does a good job, don't be afraid to say so. Send an e-mail to everyone or make sure you do it within hearing range of others. "Charlotte, your idea really made that new product work much better. That was terrific!" Being seen as supportive and offering recognition is invaluable in any workplace.

* Take action. If you see something that needs to be done, do it. If the copier needs more paper, fill it. If someone is struggling with a new system that you understand, lend a hand. Don't be a dumping ground for all the work that no one wants, but do be willing to keep things running smoothly by pitching in.

* Educate yourself. Many employers are willing to help pay for tuition or for classes that will enhance your value to the organization. Or, consider asking the boss to let you cross-train in another department to increase your effectiveness. Even by attending a weekend seminar you show the boss that you're willing to take those extra steps needed to make sure you're up on the latest trends and ideas. Be an active member of a professional organization so that the boss

knows you're staying current on what is happening in your job arena.

⋆ Be fearless. Don't be afraid to volunteer for a new project or fill in for someone else. Use it as a chance to show the boss that you're willing to face new challenges.

⋆ Ask for feedback. Show that you're open to continual improvement by asking the boss for informal feedback several times a year. Not only will this boost your chances that your annual review will go smoother but it will prove to the boss that you're open to new ideas and continually striving for improvement.

Some of these steps might be difficult for you at first if you consider yourself to be a reserved or shy person. Look for support among family and friends—they may even think of other skills or abilities you can bring to your job, and help you stay focused and confident of your new initiatives.

44. Neglecting New Coworkers

Dear Anita,

I've had my job for more than five years, and I am sick and tired of training all these new employees who come traipsing through here with no intention of sticking around longer than a few paychecks. A coworker keeps helping them, but I told her it was just a huge waste of time. They don't care two cents about us—why should we help them? Please tell my coworker she's wasting her time.

No Pollyanna

Dear No Pollyanna,

I predict it might not be wise to sabotage new hires made by your boss. My crystal ball tells me that if you keep up with the selfish behavior, you're going to get in deep doo-doo with the boss.

Anita

I once got a job at a large company, and on my first day of work, I showed up at the appointed time and gave my name to the receptionist. She began calling around, but could find no one who knew who I was or where I was supposed to go. The manager who had hired me was nowhere to be found. Finally, after I'd waited nearly an hour, the manager showed up. He barely glanced at me but sort of made a "come on" gesture that I took to mean I was to follow him.

He led me to a desk. "You work here," he said. "I'll be back."

I sat down in the desk chair. As the minutes ticked by and the manager didn't return, I became more self-conscious as other workers would glance at me and then look away. I stared into space, trying to have a calm, intelligent look on my face as if I was having really deep thoughts. The minutes ticked by slowly.

Finally, after another thirty minutes, the manager returned. He dropped some employment forms on my desk, gave me a full day's assignment load and left.

"Ask John if you have questions," were his parting words.

My immediate thought was: "Who the hell is John?"

John finally identified himself. So, by some astute questioning of him and by some divine alignment of the planets, I was able to get my work done that day.

As you can imagine, things didn't get any easier in the coming days. I finally had to ask the receptionist where the restroom was located because no one was offering the information voluntarily. I found a soda machine by tailing a coworker to its location. In my first couple of weeks, I constantly set off fire alarms by using the wrong doors and once found myself in the parking garage when I was looking for the copy machine.

It was tough being the new person. Still, after several months I was on pretty good terms with my fellow employees. They were nice folks, but deep down I never got over resenting the fact that these people let me flounder so much in the beginning. What was the reason, I wondered, for watching me crash the computer system with my mistakes and seeing me turn out a less-than-stellar product because I was unfamiliar with the process? A little bit of help from them, I thought, and I could have done a much better job earlier on.

I've had other jobs since then, and while no "first day" experiences have been that bad, I still am always surprised when some people act as if the new person needs to go through some kind of hazing ritual right out of *Animal House*. Seeing new people intimidated, scared or nervous and not offering to help is not only unkind, it's just stupid. Because if the new kid on the block can't get up to speed as quickly as possible, just who do you think pays the price?

You do. And so do your coworkers, the boss and even the boss's boss.

In the beginning of this book, I mentioned that bosses don't hire you to fire you. Well, they don't hire anyone else for that reason, either. The business world is too fast-paced and competitive for employees not to be doing their best to keep the operation running smoothly. That means that if a new employee is left to wander around Cluelessville, then someone has to pick up the slack. That might be you, it might be another coworker—or it might just fall through the cracks. But pretty soon, the problem is going to be noticed and felt by the boss.

Another thing to consider is that a new employee will not be new forever. Sooner or later, this person will get up to speed. Let's say it is soon discovered why the boss hired the person in the first place—she is an absolute whiz at designing new and innovative products. But, of course, when it comes time to pick people to work with her on a new and exciting project she doesn't choose you—because you were a butthead to her when she began working at your company. She knew you ignored her, not even bothering to explain how to work the phone system, and you definitely didn't include her when you went to lunch with your group of coworkers.

So, now who's crying into his espresso? You, that's who. Because you could have eased her road in the beginning if for no other reason than it was a nice thing to do. Nope, you were a butthead, and now you pay the price. So, as others get bonuses and promotions for working on top-drawer stuff designed by the new kid, you're still relegated to the same old job doing the same old thing. If only you'd helped her with her reports in the beginning instead of claiming you were too busy, you might be on that all-star team.

While you don't want to become attached at the hip with a new person, there are some ways to help out so that there is a payoff for the newbie, you and the boss. Try the following:

* Point out the obvious. While some companies give new hires a brief tour, it's tough to remember it all. It's always nice to introduce yourself and say, "When I go for coffee, would you like to tag along just to get another feel for where the lunchroom is located?" Then, as you pass by other landmarks, you can say, "Down that hall are the restrooms. You'll find the supply closet is also down that hall and has everything you might need in it."

* Write it down. It's always helpful if you can jot down brief information if you find a new employee struggling with something, such as computer or phone codes.

* Make the territory familiar. Offer the name of several close-by eating establishments or the cheapest nearby place to

park. Addressing the most basic needs is often the most appreciated by new hires in the early days of employment.

★ Be inclusive. Maybe a new employee prefers to eat alone, but always make the offer in the beginning to join you and coworkers for lunch. Don't forget to introduce the new person to others, and include him or her in conversations. The sooner a new hire becomes familiar with others in the company, the sooner this person will become a seamless part of the operation.

★ Be a mentor. It's never too early or too late to begin helping out someone. Mentoring is often seen as only favorable for the person receiving the advice and guidance, but that's not true. Being a mentor helps you be seen as leadership material, someone that is steady, mature, informed and skilled. Your investment of time and energy in a new person tells the boss that you're also investing in the company's success.

Remember that no one likes being the new kid. We've all been there, and it's no fun when you keep disconnecting someone every time you try to transfer a call or find yourself late to a meeting because you couldn't find the right room. So, next time you're tempted to ignore the new employee or be less than helpful, remember how it felt when you were the new kid. Go ahead and lend a hand—it's the right thing to do.

45. Fighting Change

Al Siebert says he has to laugh when he visits a local coffee shop near his house with a sign near a cash register that reads: "Afraid of change? Leave yours here."

Of course, Siebert appreciates this little joke more than most because he's director of a training organization that specializes in helping people handle change in their lives. Siebert is someone who knows from firsthand experience that a lot of employees become unhappy and tense with changes at work.

"People are in the habit of blaming their bosses or the economy for the stress at work," Siebert says. "But that's a mistake. People have to understand that what they are really stressing about is change."

Siebert says that although as humans we're designed to be excited about change and open to new ideas, we've forgotten how. As children, for example, we are enthusiastic about all kinds of new experiences because we are curious and open to learning new things. As we get older, however, we become more set in our ways and more hostile to changes, he says.

"People need to look at change as 'what can I do about it.'

It's not the situation, it's your response to it that really matters," he says.

Organizations have discovered that those who can cope with change—whether it's a new process or a new merger—have the most overall value to an employer. Those who refuse to change can so hamper an organization that they may be left behind on the career track, or even fired.

"For many decades, employers sought employees who were caretakers. That meant they wanted employees who went along, who were told what to do. They followed the job description," Siebert says. "Now, with so much change in the workplace, employers are looking for those who can reorient themselves quickly—people who adapt to change."

But let's face it: Change can be hard. People often are stubborn, opinionated and resistant to anything out of their comfort zone. Is it any wonder, then, that many managers are so frustrated with intractable employees they sometimes feel they are trying to herd cats?

It cannot be ignored that those employees who more easily accept new ideas or processes are often more valued by the boss. If your boss, for example, has to spend months getting you to fully accept and implement a new process while another employee embraces it in weeks, whom do you think he will see as costing him the most? Do you think he will appreciate your stubbornness if he has to explain to his boss why his department *still* has not fully moved toward a new goal?

It's time to look at change in a new light. Instead of seeing it as a threat, see it as an opportunity to keep growing. You need to try the following:

★ Look deep. Think about how you really feel about change. If you're really fighting it, then think about what you believe you are losing. "If you cannot handle loss in your life, you cannot have growth in your life," says Cynthia D. Scott, a psychologist and anthropologist.

★ Avoid placing blame. Being ticked at who or what has made change happen is a waste of energy. You cannot rewrite the past.

★ Open your mind. Think back to times when you were proven wrong about an assumption. For me, I thought I would never get married or like grapefruit. Well, I was wrong on at least one count: I've been married more than twenty years. There is a reason "never say never" makes so much sense. What could it hurt to be more open to new ideas or new ways of doing things? Will you self-implode? Probably not.

★ Build support. Find others in your company who seem to be more open-minded. Those who are constantly stretching their minds or abilities help create an atmosphere that makes acceptance of change easier. Don't let yourself be dragged down by the naysayers.

★ Take some risks. If you let yourself grow outside of work, then changes in your job can be easier to handle. So, go ahead. Enter that marathon you've been thinking about, take the plunge and start a jazz band or even ride the big roller coaster at the theme park. Embrace new things like you did when you were a kid.

★ Focus on learning. Just like your body, your mind must get exercise to maintain its muscle. Take the attitude that learning is lifelong and change is an opportunity to grow mentally stronger.

Change can be a scary thing. But it can also be a chance to grow and experience new things. Think of all the things you learned as a kid—how to fish, how to ride a bike, how to make sand castles. Are any of those experiences something you wish you never had? Don't look at new challenges as something to be feared, but something to be embraced. You never know when that next learning-to-fly-a-kite experience is right around the corner.

Final Note

As I was writing this book, a survey of 972 workers crossed my desk that said 71 percent of those polled would not like to be the boss. Further, not only did these folks not want to be the boss, they didn't think they could do a better job than the boss.[16]

It's easy to take potshots at the boss—just look at the phenomenal success of comics such as *Dilbert* and television shows such as *The Office*. The boss in a fictional setting often is portrayed as a complete jackass, someone who is continually rewarded for being small-minded, belligerent, hateful, narcissistic and very likely deranged. The boss is a complete and utter moron—he or she makes it impossible for anyone to get ahead.

But is that really an accurate picture? Of some bosses, yes. But after covering the workplace for decades, I also know that there are employees who are no picnic. These workers think it's OK to dress like slobs for work, squabble with coworkers like children, spend more time on the phone with friends and family than actually

[16] OfficeTeam, 2005

working and don't show up for work because, well, just because they don't want to.

So, the boss has to put up with all these issues while also dealing with the pressures from his boss. It's no wonder, then, why workers don't really want the boss's job. They see the stress a boss is under, the constant demand from higher-ups not only to personally perform better but to get employees to do the same. The same employees, I might add, who are rude to customers, have a filthy workspace and play hooky from meetings. The same workers that dig in their heels when it comes to dealing with change, tell dirty jokes and get wasted at company functions. All issues the boss must deal with.

Yeah, who wouldn't want *that* job?

Of all the letters I have received over the years in doing my syndicated column on workplace issues, I don't remember one person who ever wrote to me and said, "Boy, am I am colossal screwup. No wonder I'm not successful."

Of course not. No one sets out to mess up at work. No one says, "Gee, I think I'll take this job and see if I can't drive the boss completely whacko. What fun."

But that's exactly what happens. Someone takes a job, turns off the brain and—boom! It all starts to fall apart. The person doesn't show up on time, doesn't show tolerance for others of a different race or religion or gender, doesn't listen, doesn't lend a hand when it's needed and doesn't give a dead rat's ass about company goals.

That's when I decided that maybe employees weren't getting it because no one had ever put the rules in one place and explained why the boss cares about them. The boss isn't being a tyrant when he tells you not to use company e-mail for personal reasons. He makes that rule because it could get the company sued and then the proverbial poop would really hit the fan. The boss tells you to do certain things because there are repercussions to her career if you don't. Her boss cares that you are organized, dress appropriately and get along with others, so that means your boss is certainly going to expect you to do those things.

As I mentioned earlier, one of the things that always stands out in each of the letters I receive is that the writer believes that whatever is going wrong at work is someone else's fault. For example, I received a letter from a man who worked in a bank. He complained about his coworkers, ranting that they were lazy gossips. But in his letter, he provided details of his disagreements with them and the personal, derogatory statements he made to them during these arguments. That gave me a clue that he was at least partly to blame for the friction at work, but he saw nothing wrong with his behavior. In another letter, an employee wrote me that her boss wouldn't give her a promotion she believed she deserved. Her letter was riddled with spelling errors and grammatical mistakes, and when I pointed out that such errors at work might be holding her back, she returned a nasty reply that I won't mention here.

Such responses are frustrating to me. And if I'm frustrated by such attitudes, just think of how the boss feels who has to work with you day in and day out, watching you stumble over the same obstacles again and again. Just how long will he put up with such a performance before his patience wears thin? In a competitive business world where every employee's job impacts the bottom line, the employee who cannot correctly handle the issues I've mentioned in this book may be at serious risk of never getting ahead— or even face the possibility of being fired.

Perhaps you don't envy the boss his job, and never want to stand in his shoes. But that's no reason you have to make his job harder. He has stresses that you may never know or understand. But isn't it also true that there are many problems he has that you clearly are aware of? Take, for example, the employee who refuses to learn from mistakes, who asks for an undeserved raise or who goofs around on a business trip. Sound like anyone you know?

If so, it's time to change and quit hiding behind the "I don't knows" in your life. It's time to find the answers you need to get ahead and stop driving the boss crazy.

Begin here with this book. Before you know it, you will have tossed your bad habits and bad attitudes out the window and committed yourself to taking control of your own career and its success. And that encouraging voice you hear in your head along the way? That will be me, cheering you on all the way.

About the Author

Anita Bruzzese is an award-winning journalist whose syndicated column for Gannett News Service and USAToday.com has a readership of more than eight million. The column, one of the most popular workplace columns for the last fourteen years, is published nationally as well as internationally. It also appears on CareerBuilder.com and AOL's Find a Job.

A journalist for more than twenty years, Bruzzese has worked at several news organizations, including *USA Today* and Fairchild Publications. She was the founding managing editor of Employee Benefit News and has written for the *Boston Herald*'s Jobfind, *HR Executive* and *American Baby*. She has provided career advice through WashingtonPost.com and various workplace books. She was chosen as a CASE media fellow at Smith College and a Knight Center Fellow at the University of Maryland for business/workplace journalism. Bruzzese is also the author of *Take This Job and Thrive*.

Wake Tech. Libraries
9101 Fayetteville Road
Raleigh, North Carolina 27603-5696

WAKE TECHNICAL COMMUNITY COLLEGE

3068 0013

DATE DUE

JAN 2 9 2008		
MAR 3 1 2015		
FEB 2 1 2018		
MAR 0 9 2018		

DEC   '07